Why Not Make the Trip Worthwhile?

Chaplain Joy Le Page Smith, MA, BCC

An imprint of Pathways to Healing

Printed in the United States of America

ISBN: 978-0-692-44124-4
Pathways to Healing

Note to the reader: Every effort has been made to insure that the information contained in this book is complete and accurate. However, neither the publisher nor the author is engaged in rendering professional advice or services to the individual reader. The ideas, procedures and suggestions contained in this book are not intended as a substitute for consulting with you counselor or your physician. All matters regarding your health require medical supervision. Neither the author nor the publisher shall be liable or responsible for any loss, injury or damage allegedly arising from any information or suggestion in this book.

Biblical passages used in this book are from the New King James Version.

Dedication

To my beloved husband Gary Smith,

Sons Ted, Tim and Todd,

and to all who desire a life filled

with more peace, love and joy.

Foreword

The short articles within the book have each been published in Today's Herald-News on the Religion page, each Friday since November 1, 2019. The pandemic began soon after January, 2020, soon after Joy Le Page Smith began supplying these weekly columns.

The churches all closed, yet, here was this chaplain writing her heart out, bringing people topics that encourage, uplift, inspire and comfort. She calls it "My paper pulpit."

As a Board certified chaplain and mental health counselor, Joy writes from a wealth of knowledge and experience. She shares the joy of her soul and makes us laugh at points. At the same time she is extending what can heal what hurts in life, while showing "snippets" from Scriptures that that help people see "the Source of all hope and healing."

Brandon Bowers, Editor
Today's News-Herald
Parker Pioneer

Preface

Joy Le Page Smith, MA, writes as a Board certified chaplain who has served in hospital, hospice and jail settings for the past 25 years. As a mental health practitioner, she urges people to treasure the fact God is in their living and their loving. She reveals, here, a few brief glimpses from her own story and of her near death experiences, saying, "There is more ahead of us than behind us."

This book represents glimpses" of a typical journey through life, given its ups and downs. Readers will laugh within many of the stories while reflecting on their own experiences and thoughts.

The book reflects continually on Scripture and how one can enjoy God's guidance in their lives. Joy has offers here well-chosen, inspired glimpses of times when God's loving hand directs the lives of His children.

Readers will be encouraged to know God takes us where we are, forgiving the past and helping us "let it go." Joy writes in hopes to help people grow into themselves—advancing past where they are currently. . . As St. Paul wrote, we are being *transformed* "from glory to glory."

Each of Joy Le Page Smith's degrees are in psychology and theology. Her published books can be accessed on her website at www.healinglifespain.com, or Amazon.com.

BORN TO BE GOOD!
THE GOOD BOOK
HEAVEN'S ANGEL
CHAPLAIN JOY

By the Book . . . the essence of true love

A Chaplain's journey is often serious—and sometimes humorous. Years back, while at a party held in Scottsdale for mental health counselors, an artist was there doing caricatures. He asked me some questions, then within a few minutes—voile! I was shown on a tricycle with trainer wheels. A halo and the "Good Book" were included, along with postings of "Born to Be Good" and "Heaven's Angel."

The artist, a stranger to me, put in words what seems so true. I was "born to be good." Weren't we all? But, please note that's a trike I'm on—with trainer wheels.

Since November, 2019, a weekly column I have written for Today's News-Herald, is called "By the book." My love for "The Good Book" began when I was a child, eight years old. It was then that I found "a greater love" within which I have tried to live my life. Granted, mistakes have been made—like most everyone else—with times of being "off the path." I did try my own way at points. Still, I feel comforted by the words of a longtime friend. She said, "Joy, you have had a chaplain's heart throughout your whole life."

Board certification took place 25 years ago. What I have found is that chaplaincy is an ever-learning process through which one finds, *"It's all about love."*

While at work recently, I heard myself speaking to a patient about love. After all, when we are sick, in a strange bed—and out of control, a bit of love can help a whole lot. In a few minutes at that bedside I was able to succinctly put into words my "love philosophy:

> "We come into this world with a great capacity to love. Love is the most healing entity in the universe. And, the more we love, the more we become like our Creator who is love. In 1 John 4:8, we

are assured of this, "He who does not love does not know God, for God is love."

I recently asked an ICU patient to tell me what love has meant to him within life. He thought for a minute then remembered a stitchery his wife had made for him years ago that reads, "To love and be loved is the greatest joy on earth." After a little research, I found this quote originated from an ancient fable, yet was notably employed in a speech by Abraham Lincoln before he became the sixteenth President of the United States.

As for what I shared above, I also want to say that the opposite of love is fear. For a human the fears of not being lovable . . . not being good enough . . . or, *not doing enough* are some of the worse of all fears. Fear carries a load of torment. So, what makes us "born to be good" is the fact we are created with a conscience . . . which so often prods us to "do the right thing." And, why is conscience needed? I believe that is simply because we are here on terra firma to learn. We make mistakes—and it just happens those mistakes usually become our best teachers, helping us "wise up." I have certainly made my share of mistakes . . . have had to turn around and go the opposite direction. This is what "repentance" means.

I have read "The Good Book" from beginning to end many times and see a clear and perpetual message, "Man sins, God redeems" . . . "Man sins, God redeems." Eventually (hopefully) we get the point—that we are loved—and that love of God, self and others is what it's all about.

Do the trainer wheels come off? What does it matter? God's ongoing help, and steading hand makes the trip worthwhile. For we learn to embrace the fullness of life while working through our imperfections. God's loving forgiveness and ongoing Presence in our lives is what sees us enjoying the ride!

Does God enjoy us?

I will always remember Honeybee, shortened to "Bee" for practical purposes. This one-year-old beagle can only be described as a work of art. I simply enjoy looking at this pup. Then, of course, those multiple romps on the hillside bought absolute pleasure. But, most of the time she was on a short leash as Bee needs more training.

Surely this is over-simplified, yet I see my experiences with Honeybee as relating to the pleasure Father God must find in each of us, His children. Like the joy that must be His as He provides for us. Even perhaps some of the emotions He might have in watching our earthly antics. Zephaniah 3:17, speaks to this: "The Lord God in your midst, The Mighty One, will save; He will rejoice over you with gladness, He will quiet *you* with His love, He will rejoice over you with singing." Wow!

A soothing sight it is, just seeing my dog be her beagle-dog-self -- the creature she was created to be, one that goes a bit crazy hunting down rock chucks, chasing butterflies and rolling lustily on the sun-warmed earth. She could go through obedience school, but I love her too much. Superb as she is, she is not to become a "show girl."

This morning during my prayer time, she lay on her rug, impatiently waiting. It must have been some degree of torture, not to bolt and run. She would inch off the edge until only her hindquarters remained. Any further and Bee knew she would hear her name. Seeing her obedience—truly sacrificial—was more than amusing. There was a sense of comradery. In the short time of coming to live at the Smith house, Bee has come to know all her needs will be met. She trusts us to think of those needs even before they exist. It is now her task to earn *our* trust. And, as that grows so will her freedom. However, there are some disappointments and even brief times of anger. Yet, love always wins out, as I could never disown Honey Bee.

Observing her and realizing her simple faith in me, I begin to comprehend a little better the delight that must come to the heart of God when we put aside our fears and anxieties, speaking "peace, be still," to our sometimes quaking hearts. Like Honeybee's sigh and questioning look from the tops of her eyes as she abandons her desires in order to comply with mine. This takes trust. Similarly, our decisions to place trust in God is sure to bring results. In His timing—not ours—the exhilaration of seeing our hearts' desires will come. In the meantime, there is fellowship, albeit at times with restlessness.

Oh, how obedience must please the Father's heart. How joyous it must be to Him when we learn to sit quietly with Him and hear His voice. In the Gospel of John10:1-15, Jesus Christ is identified as our shepherd. He said His sheep hear His voice and follow Him, because they recognize His voice and will not follow a stranger. We learn to hear His voice so as not to run off to follow another's beaconing influence.

Although sheep and dogs are not at all alike in nature, this principle is still at work with each. Honeybee, much more independent, will have a harder time than the amenable lamb whose nature it is to follow. In turn, the lamb will meet with much less chastisement. Isn't that the way it is with us who are in the Kingdom of God? Some of us are hell-bent to get in trouble. Others just meekly walk along being themselves—not eager to run out to prove anything. Docile, they live on the "fat of the land," recognizing and savoring the sweet things of life that are free. Then, there are those who cower in fear, tying God's hands. It is impossible for Him to do much for folks until they learn to trust.

That "whipped pup" look Honeybee showed when chastised wrings this master's heart. I would bend down close and offer a hug. At times she turned her head and sulked, blocking my love with a grudge. Compassion saw me coaxing her out of it. Yet, sometimes for her own good I did let her wait awhile. A spoiled pup is not what I want. Nor do I want a dog that is afraid to move for fear of displeasing me.

Surely, we bring the most pleasure to God's heart in discovering the freedom of simply being ourselves. Unique creatures beautifully made inside and out. Trying to be something we are not would be a loss and surely grieve Him. Would it not also grieve Him were we to be sycophants? Scrupulously at His feet, hoping to please—ever wanting to gain His favor through good deeds— while failing to find the immense joy of leisure and fun?

Although Bee is no longer with us, it only takes closing my eyes a moment to envision her roaming the hills, finding new trails. Let's all live it, one-day-at-a-time, and simply "be." Happy trails.

Are we selling ourselves short?

The painting hung on the wall of her modest home for 15 years. Rosemary Cattrell, an Edinburgh art teacher, having no idea of its real value, decided to sell the painting for $50 to raise money for a deposit on a car. Not until then did she discover the treasure of a masterpiece, painted by the 16th-century German artist, Hans Baldung. It sold at auction for $537,000.

This could relate to us personally. Few comprehend the truth – we are originals. Stamped somewhere within is a divine signature, "made in God's image."

Every living human has a streak of genius, a prized giftedness. Millions never discover theirs, where others strike on it early, tending and nurturing the gift through using it. Like a tiny mustard seed, our gifts grow into mighty trees that yield fruit.

Some are so fortunate as to have more than one gift. Certainly, all are given for enrichment—like the arts, for the soothing of hearts. Yet, there is beauty in any job well done: butcher, baker and banker—pastor, plumber, and planner. A complete list would run the gamut from cookery to healing hands.

Even so, a mere smile from a child, such as our granddaughter, now 37 years old, who has Downs Syndrome can greatly make a difference in a person's day. Her smile is miraculous and it can change the atmosphere of a room. It grabs me; my seriousness takes leave. Without the ability to speak, she can bring a message. She brings joy to one's soul. It is strangely profound, the power this little person holds.

The rest of us have so much! How fortunate we are once our specific "genius" is found and we serve contentedly, enjoying who we are. The other option would be to envy the talents of others, without expending the effort needed to find our own. We become discontented through discounting ourselves.

Or, another blight becomes our plight through fantasies of self-importance, which can become full-blown conceit. The appetite for power and recognition soon catches us in a crafty trap of self-centeredness. This finds us telling others how to live their lives . . . working hard to make carbon copies, using ourselves as perfect models.

But Father God surely has something much better in mind. He is calling us to fully use our mental acumen. This enhances our personalities, which makes them shine with the brightness that God can give to it. We can develop our streak of genius, whatever it is, with this worthy goal in mind: To love and serve—for all we're worth. Voile! We become "good-givings" of God.

Doing this, will see us entering into joyous companionship with our Father and our fellows. Anything less is vanity. We all know it wasn't the first taste of apple juice that got human kind in trouble. No, it was an egocentric, prideful attitude signifying, "God isn't relevant. I'll do it my way."

Now, we meet a seeming contradiction. By relinquishing all concern for self-elevation, and instead let God have His way through us, His influence and essence appears naturally. We don't have to seek it . . . God brings it on. And, t is how we become lights in the world!

Yes, really believing with our whole being that we are originals, made by God, will allow the presence of Christ to be "showcased" in us *while we hardly realize it.* For all our energies, physical and mental, will be unfolding through our giftedness . . . flowing in love toward the betterment of others, known and unknown. Our joy comes through so great a privilege as to be used by Him. Consequently, we are blessed and exceedingly nourished in our spirits.

The key is two-fold: 1) staying vitally linked with our Father/Creator, fixing our "eyes" on Him; and 2) letting our hearts be perpetually brushed by love—love of God, love for ourselves and love for others. The mind, then, is not infused with self. Instead, we perpetually grow to be more like

Him in our ability to love and to forgive. This in turn allows His light to flow from us to others. Clearly, this way of being means we will learn to be humble, humble enough not to grumble in the midst of trouble, but rather to rejoice as we get through it. This brings great freedom. Bitterness, resentment, unforgiveness, envy and self-pity are bondages that we intentionally let go. These were never intended for us.

We know the saying," Let go and let God!" Rather, God's intention (*sans* disobedience) is for us to be free of these—and "Light bearers," giving all glory of God.

God's gifts are many. When he sees us savoring all He has given to us—including the beauty about us in nature and within our relationships, our essence shines. He loves us being who we are, basking in the knowledge that we are loved.

So, why "sell" ourselves short? We are priceless!

His Word is clear, "Yes, I have loved you with an everlasting love; therefore with lovingkindness I have drawn you," (Jeremiah 31:3[a]).

We gotta love that old car

After 13 years of use, the yellow/orange engine light shows up on the dashboard of our 2005 Highlander. We called it our travel car as it held oodles of luggage. Our beloved friend that has taken us so many places, far and wide, now needs a new transmission. A repair quote is $5,500 or . . . "Good-bye and adios reliable, old friend." We know that familiar dashboard readout means "trouble ahead."

We tend to drive our cars nigh unto their extinction. No interest! No car payments! What's not to love about that? Someplace within life's scene, a lot of us come to realize a little truth that goes like this: I don't know how long I am going to live, or how much maintenance I may need to see life to its end. We all love the idea of living long—with good health. There's a price tag, though. After living seven or eight decades, changes do come to both body and purse. Usually, earning power is either "gone," or greatly lessened by then. We hold great hope for our mental engines not to quake and shake, leaving us high and dry. And, we slow down a bit desiring minimal body dings and dents.

Wisdom is a great thing. And, thankfully it comes. Yes, it is there for us, no matter what age. When we reach "senior-hood," wisdom can take on a cranky voice at times, like, "Don't hit the road for a long trip in an old car."

Gary and I are still on the go and at least at times feeling "partially" invincible. Until recently, we saw a bit of the world. However, for Gary his world exists in a sphere "where the sky meets the ground."

There is a comely essence about us seniors, particularly if laughter has been a bigger part of our lives, rather than fear and anxiety. Here's one place that is truly beautiful for seniors. Most of us are at peace with death, seeing it as a natural part of having been given the great gift of a fulfilling life. We know we can't stay here forever and most of us are quite inclined to be grateful for all the living we have had. It feels great to know our "ducks are in a row," meaning a will is made, our "end of life" desires are in place—and hopefully, there is money left to ease the load for children when we take off for greater realms.

Another thing is true for most of us: We don't want to "go," yet. Ready? Yes (or we surely hope to be), but this earth can be a nice place to be . . . and we want to keep our connections. Large or small, it feels keen to enjoy what we have built here. Even for people of faith—who know heaven is waiting—this "traveling on" business is "the unknown;" it can hold some apprehension. There is a real tendency to hang onto dear ol' terra firma, thinking maybe another "tune up" is all that's needed.

I woke up one night thinking about the statement that's on our money: "In God we trust." Moving away from "that" trust, means our trust is placed on ourselves and what we can do in this life. Dr. Phil would say, "How is that working for you?" . . . especially when the earth beneath our feet begins to move. Wouldn't it be nice if our lives included a personal "dashboard," with a warning light readout of "check engine," giving us advance notice that services are needed right around the bend, allowing for a little more "readiness" for that trip to the "land beyond?" For most of us, it is always time to place more trust in the Maker . . . who has an eventual time table for His children to arrive back home, safe and sound.

There are so many passages in Scripture that comfort and lift us up—give us hope and steadfast trust that "everything is going to be OK." As Robert Browning wrote, "God is in His heavens and all's right with the world." I love this "Fatherly" advice for the road of life, "Have not I not commanded you? Be strong and of good courage; do not be afraid, nor be dismayed, for the Lord your God *is* with you wherever you go," (Joshua 1:9). Wow! How comforting. God is with us everywhere we go!

When you pray, do you listen, as well? Or, does your voice do all the talking? Listening, in hopes of hearing God is a true adventure. You may experience something close to what I "heard" early this morning, "Stay close, trust and do your best. I'm right here; you are not alone." With that message, I feel no fear. No anxiety. All *is* well, at least in my soul. And, that is where the rubber meets the road.

Now, it's time to hit the road, as there are still many miles to go! And, God will lead us as we put our trust in Him. He will bring us through. Meanwhile, staying in a stance of gratitude, no matter what comes—we are in “our most healthy place”—with fabulous rpm’s ready to move us on to wherever the road will take us. Let’s choose the “high road.”

Philanderings and 'At-one-ment'

It was early. The chill of the mountain's coming night hung over camp as I unleashed our Beagle, Honeybee, and headed up trail, planning to await the sunset. It was August, and beautiful.

Honeybee steadily traversed the hillside, yet stayed fairly close, until the summit. There, while I stood transfixed in the splendor of evening moments, she lost interest. Placing her snoopy nose to the ground, Honeybee sniffed her way furiously about the mountainside and on over the ridge. Then, when it was time to return to camp she did not respond to my call.

All the way down the mountain I whistled, called her name and waited at numerous points. No Honeybee. Choosing a sunny knoll, I sat contemplating her plight. How long would she last in the forest should her rapturous pursuit of prey carry her across several ridges and miles away? Thoughts of leaving the mountains, where we were visiting friends at their cabin, were not pleasant. Finally, there was anger that "the *mutt* was not any smarter than this!"

Slowly, I gave up hope of her coming and began walking back. Dismaying visions of her eventual demise, like stormy clouds hung in stubbornly. She could have lived out her days with every need met, love lavished upon her, enjoying many "fireside hours." But, no! She had chosen to follow her natural bent, disregarding my call, chasing off into the wilderness, in the opposite direction of protection.

On the trek back, I thought of the Father, who created us with plans for our fellowshipping together. What glorious days of enrichment would be in store could we but walk close, be obedient, savoring the sound of His voice. Is not this what King David was talking about in Psalm 27:4? "One thing I desired of the Lord, that will I seek: that I may dwell in the house of the Lord all the days of my life, to behold the beauty of the Lord

. . ." Yet, after knowing the joyous pleasure of abiding with his Creator, David, too, wandered away, satisfying his cravings.

In Psalm 51:10-12, we see his lament: "Create in me a clean heart, O God, and renew a steadfast spirit within me. Do not cast me away from Your presence, and do not take Your Holy Spirit from me. Restore to me the joy of Your salvation, and uphold me *by Your* generous Spirit."

He had found his way back to the Father's house.

There are many ways in which we "run over the ridge," one of which is that of chasing after the idolatry of having our own way. "Let go and let God," is like a medicinal dose to the human mind. Hard on the palate. The call of the wild we so often follow goes like this: "*He will wait; He will forgive ... I must explore this morsel of excitement.*" But, oh, the bitterness of tears at the pulling of "cockleburs and porcupine quills" acquired on philandering.

Some, while engaging in such wanderings, fall into the hands of cruel taskmasters, meeting with deep wounds—ragged brokenness. Escaping, finding the Father once again, clearly offered another chance. "At-one-ment" restored, brings health and trust. Oh, to be so blessed.

Much can be said for the good life of staying close, luxuriating in nurturing love, abiding in the smile of a Father who holds endless plans to enrich and fulfill. Great freedom is granted by this One who makes eminent efforts to make known the sound of His voice. He is a Father loving enough to grant the costly gift of free will. No "leashes." Random freedom of choice. All in the face of the truth that He could lose.

Thoughts of such love pervaded as I wandered toward camp that day. Coming into a clearing where the cabin could be seen, who ran to greet me but Honeybee! Dancing and switching her little body about as if she had no bones, true oblivion was portrayed. She couldn't imagine that I might be mad—but this master does not possess perfection, instead encounters fears. Fears which trigger anger. Still, joy overrode even these stubborn feelings as I was flooded with happy relief, I had not lost this beloved one.

Some stern counsel was in order. But after that we walked together on into camp delighting once again in the pleasure of one another's company. Now, with my having gained an enliven glimpse of the Father's heart.

Life—what's it all about?

Many years ago while training as a chaplain in a Phoenix teaching hospital, I faced what is perhaps the hardest of all questions. "What's this life all about?" Here lies a person whose company took a tumble. "I've tried to stay on top financially," he said, adding, "My wife left me last month and I was diagnosed yesterday with a terminal disease. How can I believe in a God who allows such misery?"

I inwardly thought, you place a lot of trust, expecting me to answer that question. There at his bedside I listened as he cried. It helped to remind myself that chaplaincy is about being a comforter—not answering questions that have puzzled the best of theologians. Today I reflect on his question, after having ministered to a multitude of patients over two decades of time.

It is a subject I have pondered many times. Actually, this man's answer can be found in the book of Job. For Job had a relationship with His Creator. He lost his health in a rapid, wretched way, along with everything he owned. Even his children were killed! He knew God alone could restore him by giving the faith, the hope and the peace he needed to go on. Amazingly, his wife complained about his ongoing faith and said, "Curse God and die." Yet, Job knew the most important thing of all was to hang onto the relationship he had with God. From the ash heap, he said, "Though He slay me, yet will I trust in Him."

In Genesis, the first book of the Bible, we see God in an intimate, loving relationship with the first people, Adam and Eve. The writer of Genesis portrays God walking and talking with theses two, loving them and instructing them to take care of the beautiful garden called Eden. All through the Bible, the message is about our being in relationship with God—and in relationship with one another.

Even today, God will speak with us when we learn to listen. How? In a "still, small voice." When I think God has spoken to me, I test it, asking myself three questions? Is what I heard in keeping with Scripture? Is it in keeping with the nature of God as I've come to know it (through "companioning" with Him consistently)? And, does it give me peace? Actually, sometimes that peace comes only after dealing with what God is wanting me to see. I lean on the truth of Titus 1:1-3, and other biblical passages, that promise God will never lead us contrary to what is written in His Word.

There is a lot to learn from Job. He held no punches as he suffered. He blasted out the pain of his soul releasing the anguish and shock over what was happening to him. He let God know how desperate he felt. God's love poured out continuously through His hearing all Job had to say. In the end Job listened, while God spoke back. Once he could grasp something of God's omnipotence, wisdom and providence, Job's confession and repentance brought full restoration.

Before his eventual death, Job's fortunes were not only restored. "The Lord gave Job twice as much as he had before" (Job 42:10). He had seven more sons and three daughters and lived to age 140. God rebuked Job's friends for their multiple dissertations. They wanted Job to accept their points of view—to shape up and get on with life. But, it was when Job prayed for his friends (forgiving them for making his trials harder) that his fortunes were restored and his life was healed.

In other words, Job got his heart in a better place in life by talking it out with God—and listening to the point God answered back. Although Scripture states Job was "blameless and upright," he came face to face with a great need to see God in a different way. It was a time of testing, which comes—even to the best of people. The book of Job is an amazing read, especially during times of suffering. Why are we tested? So, we are able to see ourselves more clearly and gain a better understanding of life, even of God.

Holy Writ shows us that this life is all about relationship. A loving relationship, because, "God is love" (1 John 4:7). That Scripture passage says that if we claim to love God, yet do not love others we are liars. Wow! That can be scary.

As it turns out, love is the most powerful entity in the universe. And, the more we love the more we become like the Creator.

The opposite is true, as we can be selfishly grasping for what we want in life, with little thought of others. We can even be outright mean, thinking nothing of stealing from others and even taking their lives before their time is up. For God has given humans the ability to make choices, through the gift of free will.

Looking at history it is easy to see there is plenty of temptation to walk away from God's love, that is until we open our human hearts to Him. Then, slowly there is a stream of tender care that can grow deep and wide. As God's love comes to us He leads us in the path of righteousness, a path that sees us living in a love relationship with God, self and others.

"For God so loved the world that He gave His only begotten Son, that whoever believes in Him should not perish but have everlasting life. For God did not send His Son into the world to condemn the world, but that the world through Him might be saved," (John 3:16-17.)

Get your hand off the rope!

Have you experienced thinking you had forgiven someone only to feel uncomfortable the next time you saw them or heard their voice on the phone? Or, struggled with no longer being able to see him or her as the loving person you once enjoyed?

There is a tenet in psychology called the "angel/devil principle," which describes the common experience of thinking highly of a person, admiring him or her until such time as you are rejected or deeply hurt by them. Then, that person can hardly do anything right.

All future actions are seen as if through smudged glass. Where there was once trust, suspicion has set up housekeeping. This occurrence is subtle, often hard to recognize for the devilish thing that it is, and no doubt falls into the category of what the writer of Hebrews warned against: a "root of bitterness allowed to spring up and defile," (Hebrews 12:15).

But what about those of us who are trying to keep our hearts clean as we continue to pray, "Forgive us our trespasses as we forgive those who trespass against us?"

What is going on when we find ourselves wanting to avoid certain people? Maybe it stems from that old self-preservation instinct that promotes the attitude, "Why let myself in for more pain?" Distance is safety, or so we think. Yet, Jesus told us to pray for our enemies. How much more so for those who were once friends?

More often than not, we have fallen into the "debts" and "oughts." One party feels the other ought to apologize, while the other feels indebted, having to live with the knowledge of pain caused.

Jesus' parable of the merciless official (Matthew 18:21-35) vividly portrays what happens when forgiveness is withheld. Author David Seamands describes in *Healing for Damaged Emotions*, ". . . this whole debt system has been built into the human personality in a most incredible fashion. There is a sense of "oughtness," of owing a debt, an automatic mechanism by which the built-in debt collectors (in the parable called 'torturers') go to work. We seek to atone for those wrongs, to pay the debt we owe or to collect the debt that someone else owes us. If we feel anger at ourselves, we say, 'I must pay in full.' Or, if we feel anger at someone else, that person must pay [or so we think.] In this way the whole inexorable process is set in motion as the person is turned over to the inner tormentors, the jailers who work as debt collectors in this awful prison."

Jesus died to set us free. It is clear that forgiveness is given, when we ask, yet with expectations for us to in turn forgive others. The "prison" of all that inner torture is therefore avoided. But, when difficult feelings persist, does this mean forgiveness has not taken place?

Perhaps no one can speak on this more aptly than Corrie ten Boom, who was imprisoned in Auschwitz, a Nazi extermination camp. There, her father and sister died as this Dutch family suffered punishment for their efforts to help Jews during World War II. In her book, *The Hiding Place*, she wrote of the difficulties in trying to forgive one of the guards who had been extremely cruel. Later, in *Tramp for God*, she wrote these helpful words: "Up in the church tower is a bell which is rung by pulling on a rope. But you know what? After the sexton let go of the rope, the bell keeps on swinging. First "ding," then "dong." Slower and slower until there's a final "dong" and it stops.

The same is true of forgiveness. When we forgive someone, we must take our hand off the rope. But, if we've been tugging at our grievances for a long time, we mustn't be surprised when the old angry thoughts keep coming up for a while. They're just the "ding-dongs" of the old bell slowing down."

How strengthening it is to know those old feelings are only echoes. Ones which in time will die out. "Peace, be still. It is forgiven," can serve as a gentle reminder to keep our hands off the "rope" when old angers surface.

Herein lies the element of patience with ourselves for being human and with the process, giving it time. Meanwhile, if the heart pounds and feelings soar in the presence of that "certain person," we are not alone. Christ stands there between us watching the struggle, waiting for us to call for His help.

The beauty of the weasel

The word "weasel" lends itself well to mental pictures. Imagine what a psychiatrist could do with such a word.

To "weasel out" is to escape duty or avoid consequences. "Weasel-eyed" describes a sly, sneaky look. Being called a weasel is getting close to "snake in the grass."

When I was a child growing up on a farm, weasels were known to raid our chicken house. Besides killing chickens, they had a canny way of sucking an egg dry, leaving the shell intact. It's an odd feeling when you pick up an empty egg.

We once had a weasel take up housekeeping in our wood pile. My father warned my sisters and me to watch out for him. "He's a fearless little critter," Dad said, "and he seems to want a fight."

So when I gathered eggs or wood, I often thought of this little animal – slender body, long head, round muzzle bearing 34 teeth. His coat was brown; not much to brag about. For his size, he was quite courageous, occasionally attacking cows and even horses.

Similar to a skunk, the weasel has glands that secrete a strong smelling substance. But I wouldn't lower myself to say he stinks.

The other day I ran across an amazing fact – even a weasel can be beautiful. With winter, the coat can turn completely white except for the end of the tail, which is black. When this happens the animal is no longer called a weasel, but an ermine. Suddenly, it becomes regal, hunted by those who wish to sport his beautiful covering. The ermine fur has long stood for the majestic. In medieval times its use was restricted to royalty. The black tail tips attached in rows became decorative trims. Ermine is very soft. If ever someone owned an ermine coat he or she was indeed "upper crust." For centuries that fur was sought, even more so than mink, as the pelts are smaller and scarcer.

Ermine are seen in Idaho, but much more plenteous further north where the winters are harsher. In fact, the further north, the better the fur.

I see a parallel between the weasel and the human person. Without faith in God's greater, loving plan for our lives we, like the weasel, can be prone to fighting, stealing, killing, sneakiness and downright meanness – out to protect our "rights" and snatch our piece of the action. But when Christ comes into our lives we begin a process of becoming purified. Strangely enough, the greater our hardships, the more opportunities for refinement. Covered with the purity of his righteousness, we become a "new creature in Christ." At baptism, we even receive a new name. But like the weasel who retains a black tail tip, we continue to struggle with the mark of sin. There is always that "little black tail" waving around, as a reminder: Only by God's grace can we become pure, "without spot or wrinkle." Through Him, the old nature of burlap brown is changed, becoming white as snow. So, when I think of the weasel I am reminded that nothing is impossible with God.

The theme might be "don't weasel out on God."

There is a lot to learn from nature

Have you ever noticed geese as they wing their way through the skies? With the exception of those who found their ways to our dinner tables, these gracious birds continue to form notable “V’s” while in flight. Have you wondered why geese fly in that formation? Scientists have discovered that the flapping of their wings creates an uplift for the bird directly behind. By flying in the “V” the flock gains 71 percent greater flying range than would otherwise be possible with each bird flying on its own.

When a goose slips out of formation a sudden drag discourages the bird from trying to “go it alone.” He quickly gets back in line where he gains the “lift” once again. When the lead goose gets tired he rotates back in the “V” while another flies point. The honking you hear is from the geese in the rear who encourage those in the lead to keep up their speed.

When a goose falls sick or wounded, two others leave the formation and follow him or her down to help. They stay to protect that goose until the bird is either able to fly again, or dies. Then, the helping geese launch out on their own or join another formation until they are able to catch up with their original group.

Nature is a great teacher. We who share a common direction, finding and following the footsteps of Christ will reach our goal quicker and easier if we travel on the thrust of one another.

As thinking human beings, it should be easier for us to help each other than it is for those within the animal kingdom, motivated by instinct only. Yet, as individuals, sometime the determination to succeed, or to gain recognition, sees us “flying” alone.

Still, deep within there lies an instinct to help the “wounded other.” We see it in the hospitals, in our churches and sometimes on the street. No doubt that was the force that motivated a father of five in New York City, which will forever stick in my mind. He jumped in front of a train in order to save an old man. On the other hand, we thinking humans often do a masterful job of suppressing that helping urge. We can find ways to appease our consciences, like, “I am late already . . . too many “balls in the air, here."

The challenge today is to reflect on how we relate to people who are hurting. They are all around us. Many are in need of food. Others are lonely, in nursing homes or home-bound long term. These are hard roads to walk. Truth be known, stepping alongside means we will be taking on some of their pain. It is so much easier to stay in our comfort zone. Yet, how can we forget the words of our Lord:

"For I was hungry and you gave Me food; I was thirsty and you gave Me drink; I was a stranger and you took Me in: I was naked and you clothed Me; I was sick and you visited Me; I was in prison and you came to Me . . . Assuredly, I say to you, inasmuch as you did it to one of the least of these My brethren, you did it to me," (Matthew 25:35-40).

All are made in the image of God. Contemplate the fact that a visit to an elderly person, a card to one who is suffering, or extending help to anyone who is less fortunate will reach the very heart of God?

Following the footsteps of Christ rarely finds us in continual ease. For sure, considering the needs of others is never easy, especially while concerned for people who live with a lot of pain, whether due to illness, grief, or poverty. Still, even when nothing else is possible, a smile with a silent prayer says, "I care."

When we go to the side of those who are wounded—those who are sinking—it must be with an ear open to God's Spirit within. Otherwise we may lack the wisdom to know when to stop our energetic flapping, our efforts to bring them back into line. Surely, it is a listening, waiting presence that allows another's thoughts and feelings to be fully heard. From those who have gone before us, we have received the gift of strength. We are called to faithfully carry the weight of that strength so as to uplift one another. It is not enough to soar on our own.

What floats your boat?

In past years, God captured my attention regarding my fears. Huge uncertainties about the future and qualms about the present seem to siphon off much of the peace and joy Jesus called the "abundant life." It is those "little foxes" of fear that can rock one's boat--big time!

The other night a dream took me on a tour of the earth. In a unique way, Father God showed me the beauties, the wonders, and the grandeur of this place called "plan-et." Within this dream, I am overjoyed with the colors, shapes, and glorious movement seen with God at my elbow.

The scene switches. God and I are sitting in a row boat together. He is rowing while I sit at the stern enjoying. We are in waters that are shallow at times and at other times so deep they seem bottomless. A sort of canyon like atmosphere surrounds us with rock formations to the right and to the left.

The stones are gigantic, exquisitely rich in color with veins of red and gold. The water is transparently clear. God and I are taking time out. I revel in His power to create such majesty in the formations of the earth. We are as one. And I am at peace.

That is until I think of what else is going on in the earth. I could see many "brothers" and "sisters" who did not want to be in God's boat. Some were playing with destructive forces found in the earth. Some were grasping for power, striving to gain prestige and reverence. Never having found love, some were in a life or death struggle to gain what they considered as the next best thing. Others were making mischief just for the sheer pleasure of it, while thriving on, or ignoring, the sufferings of others. Fear struck my heart as I sat there in the boat with God. But He rowed on, evenly watching my eyes.

Suddenly I realize what folly it is on my part to fear. What, with God so near? Wasn't He the Creator? Had He ceased to be in control? Could mere humans upset His plan? Does He not know all? See all? Is He not everywhere—always aware? How can I think for a moment that the *Creator* can *ever be thwarted* by mere, finite creatures?

Like a bubble that bursts with the touch of a finger, my fears fled. Now, I see! God is in my boat and He is at the helm! Consciously returning to the truth of His love, I am enveloped with peace. Now, to let peace reign day by day . . . hour by hour. The circumstances about me need not touch this marvelous peace, if I can only keep my thoughts from the "what ifs." With my eyes and ears open to Him, my soul becomes overjoyed in the presence of His company.

Here, I catch the simple truth. Just trust. Just believe the Father's words through Jesus His Son: "Lo, I am with you always . . ."[1] As my dream nears its end, the Father throws back His head and laughs. I cover my mouth as laughter begins to roll in me. Dare I laugh? Am I so safe as to laugh in the face of my fears?

Yes, is the resounding answer! I will laugh! I will enjoy the "ride" on this river called life, reveling in the glorious grandeur seen by the eyes—and seen by the Spirit, as God is in my "boat" and He is holding the oars.

[1] [1] Matthew 28:20 New King James Version

During those early years, I savored and enjoyed my three little boys, Ted, Tim and Todd. Yet, I feared my being sick and divorced would somehow warp their sense that life was good. Looking back, as it happened each of them became "more" not "less" because of those years in which they, too, lived with uncertainty.

But, then at age 26, I met Gary Smith. On Dec. 25, 1966, we married and the boys soon claimed him as "Dad." This man did amazing things to bring his new family through hardships that continued, right and left.

Other great things happened, like friends. I recall, years later, spending a weekend with Hilda and Nandor in Green Valley. Hilda, at 73, sensed some of my anguish. I, in turn, surmised she was someone who could hear what needed to be said. Finding an hour apart from the men, we talked. This wise woman of years was undisturbed by my tears. The essence of my lament was: "I'm tired of a body that fails so frequently. There is something I am supposed to be doing! But, it feels like I am caught in inertia!"

Hilda listened. Her words, well placed and few, went right to the heart. "What's your hurry? What are you running from?"

"Fear," I said. "Fear that my life will slip away, unfulfilled. And, perhaps I'm running from the pain of the past, old grief that seems not to heal."

Hilda, tall and stalwart, her very presence gave me hope toward waiting for God's timing. In moments of high inspiration I have been known to pray, "Make me what I ought to be, make me more like Thee … Burn off all dross that encrusts my soul." Then, comes the fire of more "waiting," more hospital trips . . . in no time at all, I inwardly scream for release.

It was once said, "There is no music in the rest, but there is the making of music in the rest."

The words of "great waiters," historically, can give comfort to us all. Job's experience of God and his lament portrays this, "When He works on the left hand, I cannot behold Him; when He turns to the right hand, I cannot see Him, but He knows the way that I take; when He has tested me, I shall come forth as gold," (Job 23:9-10).

The treasured passage in 1 Corinthians 10:13 promises that God will make sure we are not tested beyond our strength. Whatever we are going through, it is for sure God will give us a way out of it. Meanwhile, we are strengthened through enduring.

How could I know my years of struggling was the best preparation for the work I would do after raising my family. As a clinical chaplain, I feel totally "in the right place" helping people in the fox holes of life, handling pain, uncertainty, some waiting for it all to end. I can be "with them" as they wait. I can feel what they are going through. Having been through "the University of Heart-stretching Problems" I have hopes for helping them find meaning and purpose in all that life brings to them.

And, for sure, God is not finished with the process of refining my soul. Life, ideally sees us continually developing. Clearly, there are periods of time when this growth process is far from easy.

Someone once said, "When it is easy, it will be over."

The reasons we go to church

A young man recently pointed out why he doesn't attend church. His idea of church was that it exists "for people who don't have it together." Another piece of his belief was, "If you have it together church isn't needed."

So I asked him, "Does that mean we are able to determine who among us 'has it together' and who does not." At the end of our discussion we agreed that if we need to load our systems with alcohol or other anesthetizing substances in order to manage the stressors of daily life, there is something missing.

Consider what is beneath so much dependence on these substances as complicates the lives of people in our midst. The words of Augustine of Hippo written in 397 A.D. are as true today as they were when he wrote them, "Because You have made us for Yourself and our hearts are restless till they find their rest in Thee."

It is wonderful to experience the goodness of God. Attending church services and study groups is where faith is explored. Individuals enjoy camaraderie while discovering Biblical truths.

Jesus' message reveals the greatest of all commandments, "'You shall love the LORD your God with all your heart, with all your soul, and with all your mind.' This is *the* first and great commandment. And *the* second *is* like it: 'You shall love your neighbor as yourself.' On these two commandments hang all the Law and the Prophets,'" (Matthew 22:37-40).

Without a doubt, it is easier to live out these two commandments while being in communion with others who are on the same spiritual quest.

Church attendance powerfully affects lives through promoting an understanding of how to encounter God. We find we can talk with Him—and hear His message to us. Besides coming to know how very loved we are by God, attending church promotes a feeling of identity and harmony, as we share our lives with others.

The question of who "has it together in life," or, who is successfully living out those two grand commandments of God, can never be fairly determined. Yet, the conversation with the young man found me wanting to answer the question, "Why go to church?"

Actually, there are countless blessings as Harold G. Koenig points out in *The Link between Religion and Health*. It contained numerous gold-standard research studies conducted by various examiners reporting on what they call "the faith factor." Their studies revealed a link between having the best of health and the practice of attending church services frequently. Once the research was compiled, it became clear that twenty-one well-documented benefits are proven to be gained by people who maintain devout spiritual beliefs and attend church. These include:

Social support,

Less loneliness,

Less anxiety,

Less depression,

Less negativity in speech and thoughts,

Healthier behaviors,

Better health,

Less need for alcoholism and recreational drugs,

Less sex outside of marriage,

Fewer suicides,

Better coping skills,

Greater generosity (with time and money),

Increased hope and optimism,

Better resilience while experiencing difficulties,

Far less fear of death.

It is clear to me that fewer people have self-esteem issues when they attend church frequently. At church we are surrounded with strong, courageous individuals who are making a difference in our community and in our world. Learning to trust and follow the promptings of one's heart brings accomplishments, which bring fulfillment and a sense of life being full of joy.

Church attendance brings more meaning to life. While building spiritual endurance, it instills hope for eternal life. In humility, we admit our need for others. (Otherwise, we could stay home and stream sermons.) For sure, we are most able to stand strong and faithful within the experience of sharing the journey with others—particularly those who know to call on the Lord for help during difficult times.

I learned early in life that prayer and worship greatly fortifies the soul. It gave me empowerment to get through difficulties of life and even to rise above them. We need each other, as believers, to reach that transcendence, especially when push comes to shove. Life surely does have a way of "bringing it on" overshadowing plans, jangling our lives, and threatening our sense of Shakespeare's "all's well in the world."

Having a devotion to God sees us choosing friends who support and encourage us toward our goals of living what Jesus referred to as "the way."

Come Sunday, church goers want to be right there on those benches called "pews." It's "in the pews" where we get the good news.

More likely than not, we leave with a strong sense of "all's right with my soul."

The power is ours!

Did you know that positive thinking *positively* changes the chemistry of our bodies? We learn about this through a field of medicine called psychoneuroimmunology*, an aspect of medicine that deals with what is taking place in the mind, the will, and the emotions of each one of us.

This long word indicates that everything that goes on in our psyches affects our neurological system, our immune system, and our endocrine system. Later, the scientists found the hormonal system is also affected either positively or negatively by our thoughts. That is why the asterisk is added. Apparently, making the word any longer than psychoneuroimmunology wasn't advisable.

The body is equipped with amazing intelligence. It is continuously at work fostering stability, balance and healing within our many organs, systems and tissues. Still, we can disrupt that process, simply through the way we think. Fear, anxiety, negativity are three major culprits. Yet, perhaps the worst are bitterness, hatred, and thoughts of revenge. Unhealthy thoughts are without doubt enemies of good health.

Other enemies to our good health are more familiar, like poor eating habits, not getting enough rest, smoking, heavy drinking and taking drugs other than those prescribed by doctors. These are things we can do something about. Yet, the hardest of all may well be controlling our thoughts.

In my work, it is evident that a large percentage of people are giving minimal thought to the very large role spirituality plays in wholeness. Truly, the soul is most wholesome when we have a concept of who we are, what our gifts are and why being here on the globe matters.

The happiest people on earth are not those with clever jokes, entertaining us—or the people with "a lotta money." No, the happiest people on earth have discovered a life that is meaningful, one that holds purpose. They most often are those who have concluded "there is a God"— One who loves them through and through . . . the One who has allowed this experience of life. Great enjoyment comes in finding God is fully present to us.

There are remarkable scientific facts indicating that we are created to enjoy this life. Yet, many do not. Rather, they are simply trying to numb out with alcohol and/or opioids hoping to escape how bad they feel. Not only do 200 people die daily from overdose in the US—but now our suicide rate is climbing.

It is always good to look closely at this truth: We are spiritual beings having a human experience. Believing we humans are here to do whatever bangs our shutters, gets us into major trouble.

Within my 25 years of doing mental health counseling, I ask within the first session, "Why do you think we are here?" Some don't even want to think about that question. A few say, "I don't know." But, mostly I am given an answer that rings amazingly true for the majority. After giving it some thought, most say, "We are here to help others." Or, "We are here to learn." They come for help when their lives are upside down, but, while thinking deeply and looking inward, they innately know what life is really, truly about.

Take the word "psychoneuroimmunology." It is the study of the connection between the psyche and the extent it can affect the very cells and juices of our bodies. The word "psyche" is synonymous with the word "soul." This may clarify why our beliefs, thoughts and emotions play a significant role in our body's ability to stay well. In my studies, I discovered a seldom realized precept: Feelings follow thoughts. So, when you feel rotten, ask yourself, "WHAT WAS I THINKING!"

Holy Writ supports wholesome thinking throughout. Philippians 4:8, gives the nutshell version, "Finally, brethren, whatever things are true, whatever things are noble, whatever things are just, whatever things are pure, whatever things are lovely, whatever things are of good report, if there is any virtue and if there is anything praiseworthy—meditate on these things."

Medical doctors can do wonderful things for us when we get sick. But when it comes to thoughts and emotions—we are in control. We hold the power to take dominion over what can rob us of one of the greatest pursuits of life: good health!

"You will keep *him* in perfect peace, w*hose* mind *is* stayed *on You,* because he trusts in You. Trust in the LORD forever, for in YAH, the LORD, *is* everlasting strength," (Isaiah 26:3-4).

Courage is the beginning of wisdom

Her eyes were a mixture of fear and sadness as my friend spoke, saying, "There is a tumor… the doctor has decided against a needle biopsy saying one in five of this type are cancerous." "Eva" sought help at a hospital in California.[2]

Three weeks later, we talked again before surgery. This time there were no tears. She spoke of knowing that she was in God's hands and marveled at the peace she felt. Her eyes were bright, no longer dark with fear.

A young man, "Fred," with a wife and two small children grew quiet and helpless as he watched the economy worsen. One after another of his co-workers was laid off. He had worked there the past ten years believing the job held a promising future. It was now nearing bankruptcy. He knew company policy would require his discharge before other employees who had worked longer than him.

The stress showed on Fred's face when my husband and I visited him with his family. The children were running and laughing through the house, unaware of their father's plight. A few weeks passed before we talked again. I dialed the phone with a little hesitation after not being in touch for several weeks.

"How's it going, buddy?"

His answer came across the line with exuberance. "Everything's great. Just great."

Thinking something had changed with the company, I said, "Going great sounds good. Changes at work, huh?"

His voice grew quiet, but full of assurance. "It's the same. I just don't worry about it now." He, too, was well ensconced in a walk of faith. Soon

---

[2] Fictitious names are used in this writing.

after, he had a new job, this time doing what he loved.

Another instance of witnessing faith at work, involved a friendship between a young woman who I will call "Sue" and her friend, "June." Sue, who at the time was my coworker, spoke of the friendship between them becoming more and more uncomfortable, "like a pair of pinching shoes," she said.

"More recently," Sue said, "I have cringed over certain behaviors that trip me up as I try to communicate with her, but now June is unwilling to handle even a request for clarification. I am exhausted with it all. I can't say anything right; and, I am often confused by her retorts. Gulping down my feelings is no longer a good choice for me."

Eventually, these experiences rendered the relationship into one of forced congeniality.

"Everything was "rosy"—or so it seemed, Sue said, "But all we have is surface talk, now." Nothing heartfelt is shared like we used to enjoy."

No doubt they both were hurt by what was happening. And, Sue could not seem to get things back to where they were in the friendship. She admitted steaming inwardly as if from an inner pot of simmering resentment. The relationship was stuck as Sue gave up all hope for honesty. Ambivalence had forced them into silence. And, the inability to be honest tore them apart.

Finally, Sue made up her mind not to allow herself to be manipulated into guilt, but rather to state she needed to stop trying to be understood. Sue knew more than likely the friendship enjoyed with June in the past would end . . . and so it did.

I see all three of these life stories as having two things in common. Each required courage to get through adversities. But there is something more. Each of these three individuals lived prayerfully and had a treasured relationship with the Lord. They prayed for guidance and sometimes spoke of their experiences with friends who could listen as they tried to figure things out.

Within these three incidences, there was pain and apprehension in the areas of health, income and relationship. Yet, each person eventually found the strength needed to move forward by relying on God's help. Having done so, courage resulted, bringing strength to overcome difficult circumstances and to accept their outcomes.

Someone once said, "Courage is fear that has said its prayers." After reflecting on some of my own life's experiences, I know this is true. At times we cry out to God in great fervor. We "get a hold of the horns of the altar," as an Old Testament writer put it. We "hang in there, persistently trusting until peace comes along with a resolution. We gain courage—in the midst of what can be exasperating circumstances—and strength.

We rely on one of Christ's last promises before leaving the earth for heaven, "My peace I leave with you. My peace I give to you." He knew when He spoke that some of his followers would go to the grave as martyrs, and that each would go there with peace. He Himself led the way. It is a peace that is miles apart from resignation and worlds away from fatalism. It is something mighty—that makes our faith worth living—and dying for. It is a faith that holds us together. This kind of faith doesn't just touch us deeply, it supports our progress in gaining *wisdom* and the determination to keep growing.

Holding fast to faith gives courage through the challenges of yesteryears, and is now providing courage within the tests and contests of today. Scriptures continuously builds and fortifies faith, strength and courage through admonitions like, "Trust in the Lord with all your heart, and lean not on your own understanding; in all your ways acknowledge Him, and He shall direct your paths," (Proverb 3:5-6).

Don’t neglect having fun

Some years back, our adult son, Tim, stayed in our home. When we returned he said, “Mom, I loved being here. Everywhere I looked I saw you and Dad—your things, all that represents you is here.”

He went on to say it made him think of how the personality of God is seen everywhere in nature. We talked of how it feels to take a “joy” walk without thinking, just feeling the sun, the wind; hearing the birds and sounds of children at play; smelling the earth’s aroma; taking time to touch the smoothness of a leaf or live moss on a rock. The next best thing to being with the Father. Pleasure-filled moments. A form of play?

I am a fine one to write about having fun—just a beginner then and even so today in learning how to live a life less tightly structured. Yet, the more I am into prayer, listening to God, the more I feel invited to relax and enjoy the earth and its people, living more spontaneously.

When we lived in Idaho, efforts to rediscover play saw me asking Gary to build a swing in the backyard, which was a hillside. He built a splendid swing with two seats. Then, in the cool of the evening, we would swing together, out over the hillside, thrilling at the view below.

Children are not the only ones who need play. At any age the human spirit longs for adventure and recreation. Watch children who have not yet learned there are chores to be done. In love with life, they laugh, tickle, skip, sing, run, dance and jump. Early in life, most children are full of love for life.

Dr. William Diehm, psychologist/author, claims those are the actions of people who are in love. He said, “Do you want to recover the feeling of love? Then act that way. Don’t say you can’t.

"People have been acting brave when they feel fearful, and acting nice when they feel mean, since the beginning of time. It is not hypocritical; it is a method to recapture feelings by deliberately having fun."

Adult forms of play—from tennis to table games—do not always rest the soul. They may peak in a fit of competition or aggression. It is hard to determine what "true play" is and what is not? But, the *feeling* you have while engaging in an activity is the determining factor. If you feel light-hearted, happy and renewed while working in your garden, it is feasible to consider that a form of play.

I will never forget seeing my 80-year-old grandmother take off her shoes and walk through summer's grass. She told me of looking in the mirror and saying, "Is that old lady me? Inside, I feel 19!" Her words were surprising as this lady often complained of her arthritic pain. Yet, in her heart she still loved fun.

A close friend and I decided recently when we are 80, we will go skipping hand in hand through the park. After a good laugh at the thought of it I said, "We'd better do it now while we can."

Truly, the greatest fun I have found is seeing laughter in the face of another. No doubt this is why light-hearted teasing is fun. But have you noticed the ubiquitous temptation to hurry right on, stifling even the slightest grin? We take ourselves too seriously!

For the next three months, I intend to immerse myself in summer, taking time to find some fun. I hope you will do the same. Then write and tell what you discover!

Oh, by the way, I reached such a large number on my birthday last month that you might not see me skiing, or wave surfing on the lake! Going barefoot in the grass may have to suffice.

Watch for it . . . you will come to it, by-and-by. And—there will still be plenty of fun to be had for all those who are young at heart.

Those of us who have had many birthdays can also look forward to many blessings:

"The silver-haired head is a crown of glory, if it is found in the way of righteousness, (Proverbs 16:31)."

"Blessed is the man who trusts in the LORD, and whose hope is the LORD. For he shall be like a tree planted by the waters, which spreads out its roots by the river, and will not fear when heat comes; but its leaf will be green, and will not be anxious in the year of drought, nor will cease from yielding fruit," (Jeremiah 17:7-8).

The Power of Grandparents

My Grandmother Margret chewed tobacco. She grew up in Arkansas in the early 1900s at a time when most teenagers savored this practice. But Grandma continued this into her old age.

Certainly, this was a questionable behavior for us, as her grandchildren. Inwardly, we "closed our noses" while seeing her use her spit can. But I enjoyed my grandmother. She loved having me comb her hair and just be with her. She mended clothes and crocheted from mid-life on. The greatest thing about this grandmother is that she loved God and was quietly prayerful. She always went to church—in fact she helped found a little church in Boise, Idaho, on Main Street while beginning her family of eight children.

Her husband, "Grandpa" Butler, was a logger at that time. He did not approve of Grandma's "religion." In fact he hid her shoes so she would not go to church. But Grandma went anyway, in her bare feet. His objections to her faith were definite until the time when a tree fell on him, after which an angel stood on the stump and preached him a sermon. From that time on this Grandpa went to church with Grandma into his old age.

I will pause for a moment to tell you about my Grandmother Mary, on my mother's side. She too was wonderful, a mother of 12 children of French lineage, the family dating back to the times of King Louis XIV. Her forefathers migrated into Québec in the 1600s. Although I have not traveled there I have a picture of a statue erected in honor of that family as Germain and Reine Lepage (brothers) were early settlers of Québec, able people, notable contributors.

This grandmother certainly had our attention and our respect. She too went to church regularly, alone without her husband. She was a quiet person, always putting others ahead of herself. I only remember one conversation with Grandma Mary. I was about to be married. She gave me this tongue-in-cheek advice, "Have a glass of water at bedtime— and nothing else." I knew exactly what she was saying . . . still, I did my part for posterity, by birthing three sons within the following decade.

There is no comparing these Grandparents. Each of them taught me the importance of family and of sacrificing for one's family. These messages came through observing them, as I have no memory of them giving advice, aside from that "glass of water at bedtime" noted above, given with Grandma's defining nod. How they lived their lives with love for God and love of family brought considerable knowledge and a certain wealth to my soul.

With Grandma Mary, who hardly ever spoke at all, I learned the power of presence. I came to understand the importance of silence. Especially, at meals where it was mostly about digesting our food. Grandma Mary was a master of silence. (As for me, I continually pray to practice a little more of this.) Grandparents have powerful roles in the lives of children and grandchildren. Whatever they do or do not do— these are notable people—prominent in what they achieve for society by simply being loving people! Of course not everyone succeeds well as a grandparent. These, too serve as examples of how *not* to be in this world.

Another lesson I learned from my grandparents was to be hard-working and to care very much about those who are outside your own family. My Grandfather Henry had a large grocery store, was cheated out of his business by a brother. He then started a small neighborhood grocery next door to his home. Grandad was known for feeding families on credit. I was once told by a schoolmate, at a class reunion, of how her family made it through the depression because of my grandfather. He did not go to church but he did exemplify the teachings of the Bible through the way he lived. Grandad was very much loved by all in the family. His work at the store was endless, but he still took time with his grandkids, teaching us how to play cards. Yet, we could never play on Sunday. That was his rule.

Why tell of the snus habit of my grandmother maintained? Well, I think Grandma Margret would want me to do so if it could help others "get a clue." We who loved her looked beyond what was ugly and saw all the beauty in her. Maybe that is the way we should look at ourselves, while doing our best to get past our "uglys." Could it be God has great joy, in being within our souls, regardless of what we have not yet overcome? Maybe He is watching us like little children learning to dance. We miss a lot of steps, yet keep going! He sees what we accomplish in spite of it all. In the long haul what God sees is the good, while pulling for us to "stay in the light"—and keep pressing towards being our best.

There is lots to be said about not judging one another, while keeping our minds on what we can improve in ourselves. Grandma's faux pas was right out there in front for all to see, pretty much continually. Conversely, most of us struggle secretly with ways in which we know we could do better. But hiding what can bring shame is definitely hard on our health, both physically and spiritually. It is important to know those who truly love us overlook the fact we are not perfect. This is giving one another grace. When we judge another, it means we don't truly love them.

I believe both of my grandmothers were "saints." Yet, I was closest to Grandmother Margret because she shared her heart. She talked of her faith. The fact she also lived it was evident, plus the whole family always knew this dear person was praying for us. Before she died she told me of her practice of praying every day for all members of the family by name. That would be a lot of names! Since then I've worked at carrying her tradition forward. Her portraying, through word and deed, what it is to be a Christian resulted in nearly every one of her grandchildren and great-grandchildren becoming people of faith. I learned from her that it pays to speak up about matters of faith—and to do one's best to bring our families all the way to heaven's gates through keeping them in our prayers.

"Love suffers long and is kind," (1 Corinthians 13:4).

Fortunately, almost all grandparents know how to love little kids. What a powerful influence that becomes!

O' death, where is your sting?

Years ago my friend Marge's teenage son was killed while skiing with friends and classmates at Bogus Basin Ski Resort. He accidentally skied into a tree and was killed instantly.

That night after my friend received the news in her home I witnessed astounding faith.

"Tommy is with God," she said through her tears. "He is now praying for us."

She was suffering all the feelings of shock and unbelief that Tom could be taken from their home so suddenly, but the overriding theme flowing from Marge that night was one of trust and assurance that God would bring meaning to Tom's death.

A Mass was scheduled the following morning at Bishop Kelly High School for a grieving student body, along with the family. Marge said, "Jim and I cannot go. But it would make me happy if you would go."

The gymnasium was filled with students, friends and faculty. Tom had been designated "Outstanding Sophomore of the year." He was a treasured person. The fact of his distinctive acumen was born out by more than words.

Words. Many were said and surely they comforted. No doubt each came away with some nugget of truth. For me it was Father William Dodgson's words: "Tom's life is changed. But it is life . . . it is the Father's life. This is a time when Tom would want you to make your faith work."

I was reminded of words said by another man of God, C. S. Lewis, as he grieved the death of his wife, after their marriage of only four years. He wrote:

"Bridge players tell me that there must be some money on the game 'or else people won't take it seriously. ' Apparently it's like that. Your bid—for God or no God, for a good God or the Cosmic Sadist, for eternal life or nonentity—will not be serious if nothing much is staked on it. And you will never discover how serious it was until the stakes are raised horribly high; until you find that you are playing not for counters or for sixpences but for every penny you have in the world. Nothing less will shake a man—or at any rate a man like me—out of his merely verbal thinking and his merely notional beliefs. He has to be knocked silly before he comes to his senses. Only torture will bring out the truth. Only under torture does he discover it himself."

Sources reveal Lewis, author of *The Chronicles of Narnia* and many other famous titles became an atheist at age 15. He later described himself as being paradoxically "very angry with God for not existing and equally angry with Him for creating a world." The "how" and "why" of that part of his life can be seen in *The Conversion Story of C.S. Lewis*.

Grief is torture. It strikes us cruelly, ripping away the peripherals, giving us a long look at our nakedness. It is human life that is at stake. We grapple with the meaning of life and death, coming away like Jacob of the Old Testament, injured but blessed with new appreciation for life's essence. Blessed in the realization that each one of us is mortal, and a reminder not to take people for granted.

Time seems to stand still while we grieve. It is a time for "verbal thinking" and "notional beliefs" to make that long journey from head to heart. Often faith is weighed in the balance and found wanting as we cry out, "Lord I believe . . . help my unbelief!"

While caught in the throes of grief sometimes we cling to God for our strength and solace and other times we throw our anger toward God, attempting to empty ourselves of the burden. But if we refrain from turning our backs on God—if we wait, watch and listen instead of running—we will encounter His response, the long loving gaze of a Father who also has suffered. A Father who understands.

The funeral of a friend of Gary's and mine was held last night. We were unable to make the trip to our hometown to attend. Today, through tears my sister related things about the service for this wonderful, friend who lived an exemplary, Christian life. Loved by many of us, for sure.

His wife Letty is very close with my sister, Mary and her husband, Dave. She related much to them within Jim's final days and his last words.

Letty said, "Jim was very sick until he quit treatment and entered hospice. But, he could not take morphine. We prayed he would not suffer—and, after that he had no pain. She told of his last day being at rest in bed when suddenly a very big smile came over his face. He exclaimed, "Letty, bring some chairs in here! There are so many angels and they are all standing." Immediately thereafter, Jim passed over from this realm into Heaven's incalculable transcendence.

John 14:1-2, tells us, "Let not your heart be troubled; you believe in God, believe also in Me. In My Father's house are many mansions; if it were not so, I would have told you. I go to prepare a place for you. And if I go and prepare a place for you, I will come again and receive you to Myself; that where I am, there you may be also. And where I go you know, and the way you know."

How wonderful are the truths of Scripture. Nothing can truly uplift us so thoroughly as Scripture can, because it touches our spirits.

The softer side of grief

On an early Sunday morning, while away from home, I pondered with awe the beauty throughout the Basilica of the National Shrine of the Immaculate Conception in Washington, D.C.

Many things there spoke of the power and presence of God. The hardness of marble altars, stone floors and wooden pews spoke of strength. Then I looked at the people. They were soft. Vessels of earthen clay, yet filled with spirit.

Many shy away from being called "soft." But the softness I saw was holy. That which makes us vulnerable, malleable and capable of love.

Back home this truth was clearly seen when I visited the home of friends who had just lost their 24-year-old son in death. Neighbors, family and friends from their parish came, some with arms loaded with food. Many offered prayers from caring hearts. And as they left each carried away a piece of the pain. So much pain to be borne there in that home. Yet the grieving family knew through the people that they would not be bearing this alone. The softness of human love was leaving its impact, as love in action extends strength.

At times like this we often feel inept. Words may seem inadequate. But what we do have to give is enough. That is empathy, wrapped in flesh. When we are weak, then we are strong. Why? Because of our dependence on the Lord, rather than on ourselves. The Apostle Paul exhibited that throughout the letters he left for all of us believers who follow "the way," which Christ revealed through His teachings.

When we see a fellow human hurting, something incredible occurs. There is an urging within to stop—set aside what we are doing—and go. "Be there." It is love in action, coming from the treasure of one's heart. Tears convey release, as solace is received. Such "holy water" grants clear vision that this love, as it flows from others, is a healing force.

We all endure grievous trials during this life. 1 Peter 1:7, portrays how it is through these hardships that our faith comes forth "much more precious than gold that is tested by fire." So, we are in a refinement process and if we yield ourselves to it, enrichment results. And, God is praised.

While alongside my friends, I saw no anger or resentment. No bitterness spouting, although these dear people had lost another son a mere 13 months before. God is their ally, not their foe. Softness is felt. Tenderness and, peace reigns. Philippians 4:7, refers to this as "the peace of God, which surpasses all understanding, will guards our hearts and minds through Christ Jesus."

So here we are as humans, ideally all "soft covers"—no "hardbacks." Fragile, destined for much wear and tear. Yet durable beyond comprehension. Filled with strength, having quite enough to share.

People. Earth's richest resource. Vessels deemed worthy by God to carry His love. A love experienced most vividly when seen flowing from one to another. Oh, holy ones of God, we belong to each other.

Thank God for our hearts of flesh, capable of expanding, stretching, growing—even at the risk of breaking. Yet it is in the breaking that we are formed afresh. As Christ's body, broken in the Eucharist and given away for the nourishment of many, we live on loving life and one another. The "breakings" do come, challenging our souls and in the end, what is remembered is that faith does hold strong when we depend on the power of the Spirit. This is what makes us more than flesh . . . And able to live forever.

Is this our biggest challenge?

For decades ours has been a "death denial society." We pretend death isn't viable for us. It's "Out of sight, out of mind." We live on the edge of denial, with death seeming to be something that happens to others. Attending funerals can present elements of inner angst that some prefer to avoid "like the plague." Well, now we have a plague, here in 2020-2021. One that is pandemic, prevalent throughout the entire world. (Please God, make it end!)

We cannot avoid thinking about death as the numbers of those who die from the COVID-19 virus are astounding. This fact prevails as we read the newspaper, or view the news. People are fearful—and this is not good. A study of muscle testing (kinesiology) suggests our muscular system is weakened when we know something is wrong for us, or we face a threat. It may be possible our immune systems are also weakened as we begin to realize the truth, "I could catch this COVID thing—I could die from it." Perhaps we are less likely to become sick with the virus if we conquer the fear of it?

It is possible to make friends with death and come to live with the truth that death is part of life. It is for sure, none of us will get out here alive (at least in a temporal sense.) One of the greatest mysteries of all is that we are here on earth for a short time and that none of us know how long we will have here. This is the very factor that makes life so precious.

Embracing death, learning to accept it as a friend can make a huge difference with our quality of life. If we know it's "there for us" as friend, not a "foe," we are more apt to have peace and take care not to bring death on early. Of course, we had best not do something stupid, like racing a car or motorcycle at excessive miles per hour . . . or, driving while intoxicated. Clearly, there are many other ways in which we can bring on death before it needs to come. Life is too precious not to pay *close attention* to how we live, how we take good care of ourselves in order to live long.

Why Not Make the Trip Worthwhile

For twenty of my early years, I had a hard time staying alive until a life-saving surgery was invented near my 35th birthday. This was a miracle for me as it stopped blood clots flowing from my legs and abdomen into my heart and lungs. Now, my living long astounds me . . . when there is time to think about it.

How I made friends with death was through journaling, a practice that kept my mind on what I truly wanted to happen while here on earth, with God's help. The Bible became my daily guide, allowing me to become more "spiritually minded," with prayer flowing easily and often.

Death became my friend by making it a part of how I live my life. Perpetually grateful for being alive, I celebrate life by giving thanks to God for the opportunities to help others on their journeys. One of the greatest of all blessings for a chaplain is to be there for individuals as they manage their fears in life and as they face death.

As regards handling the difficult emotions of fearing one's end-of-life, it does no good to deny the fact that it will come. Dealing with that fear of it, honestly and squarely, takes a trust in God's provision of everlasting life. Jesus came to be with us in order to provide our eternal future with Him. This world is our pilgrim-place. We will truly be alive in the "ever-after" once we are at home with God who created us. Meanwhile," to be spiritual minded supports a meaningful lifestyle wherein there is peace.

One of the good things that can come out of this pandemic is that most of us are living at a slower pace. Another, is that we see more clearly our temporal state. These factors prepare us better for "making the best of it," while here. We can determine what we want to achieve in life, then get to the job of making it happen. Reading the Bible daily. (Perhaps starting with the book of John.) And, seek a church where you can gain ongoing growth in Christ.

Keeping our hearts in God's truth brings wonderful peace and comfort. "Always ready" becomes the best possible motto for life, while here on terra firma. What awaits will be glorious, beyond what we can imagine.

A little trip to the ditch . . .

When our son, Ted, was six years old, he was intrigued with the Bible story of Peter walking on water. With childlike faith he headed for the irrigation ditch to give it a try. But born in the space-age Ted knew something about backup systems. He wore his galoshes.

When Ted became a man he told me of his little trip to the ditch and how hard it was on his faith. I'm glad to see him as a grown man, along with his brothers, faithfully "walking on waters" in a spiritual sense. I wonder how Peter must have felt. Under the best of circumstances—in the physical presence of Jesus—his faith moved right out from underneath him.

The trials we face day-by-day are not the same choppy waters that Peter tried to master, but the test is the same. Peter took his eyes off Jesus and looked at the circumstance. It was doubt and fear that flooded out his faith. The question is, how to keep our eyes on the master when the storms are raging? How do we have faith when the "waves" are high and mighty?

First, what is faith? Hebrews 11:1 shows us that "faith is the substance of things hoped for, the evidence of things no seen."

This means faith is holding fast to something even before we see it happening—mentally picturing our answer and saying "thank you" although it is not yet a fact. Faith is all wrapped up in what's holy, and although challenging, it is wholly obtainable.

So, where do we get faith? Romans 10:17, explains that "Faith comes by hearing,

Through faith we move within a storm to a place of peace, on top of the "waters" waiting the storm out.

Unfortunately, we don't always do that. We get stressed up, toss and turn in the night and sometimes get an ulcer. Then, just as the Master reached out to save Peter before he sank into the dark waters, our Lord rescues us. But not before we uttered Peter's cry, "Lord, save me." Our Lord knows we are weak—and he loves us, lifting us above our struggles.

The Psalmist knew what it was like to be nearly overwhelmed by the waters of affliction as he wrote: "all your waves and billows are gone over me." Then, said, "He brought me up also out of the horrible pit, out of the miry clay, set my feet upon a rock and established my steps," (Psalm 40:2).

To use another analogy, could it be that we have one foot on the rock and the other on shifting sands? Is this why some of us are experiencing "the pits?"

Faith brings new vision. Vision without the limitations of physical sight allows us to see beyond the storm of the moment. The apostle Paul intended this when he admonished us to "walk in the Spirit."

Strangely enough, it is often the little things that ripple the waters of life. Thoughtless words and actions trip us up. So often it is our pride that hurts the most. But it is false pride that makes us think "we cannot make mistakes." Phooey.

Clarence J. Enzler wrote in *My Other Self,* "Should your imperfections momentarily gain the upper hand, you do well to be displeased at your fault . . . . When you allow yourself to be dejected over your involuntary faults, it is because you think you are better than you really are. And once you allow your imperfections to upset you, you are likely to find yourself in a sharp tongue, irritable mood in all that you do."

God has faith, too. Faith in us. Instead of seeing us as we are now, He sees us as we will be when His work is finished within us. We must have faith in ourselves, too, knowing that he is working with his best tools at the safest speed to bring us into what He would like us to be . . . people who are fully trusting in Him.

God does not get frustrated with us. Instead, he is there to help us when we want to bail out on ourselves.

We have a lifetime to overcome our every innate weakness. Each time we succeed in resisting the temptation to go our own way we are stronger for the next go-around and each time we keep our eyes on the Master in the middle of the storm, faith grows.

Taking time for the ‘fun things’ in life

A “Serendipity” serves to describe an unexpected moment of happiness or felt pleasure. These come, surprising us with laughter, or an uplift. They can easily be missed, as serendipities call for stopping what we are doing to delight in them.

Gary and I experienced a surprising happenstance while on vacation years back. We still can stop to savor it. We were hiking in Ecola Park, at Cannon Beach, Oregon, when we passed an older man on the trail. He asked Gary, “Do you have the time, Sir?” Both of us looked at our watches as Gary gave him the time.

That proved to be the beginning of an astounding encounter. As it happened, this man turned out to be anything but ordinary. He was elderly, appearing to be a little unkempt but fit enough to take to the trail. It was his spirit that took us by surprise.

Conversation sparked and some of his words still come to mind even as years have passed. Without mentioning God, this man told us much about Him, inadvertently answering questions I had sorely pondered.

Tears surfaced when the “old man of the trail” spoke of how joy is to be at the bottom of all we do—that “fun” is at the base of the word “function”—and how we can go as far as we want to go, see as much as we want to see and experience as much as we want to experience while riding through life on the crest of joy.

As if talking was not enough, the man asked, “May I sing?” We were happy to let him. He began singing in a different language. Then he sang in English to the same melody, now stretching out his hands as if to include nature. It was a phenomenal experience right there at the edge of the Pacific Ocean!

I began to wonder if he was a real person or perhaps an angel. Were we being "entertained unawares," as happens to people at times. Hebrews 13:2, says, "Do not forget to entertain strangers, for by so *doing* some have unwittingly entertained angels."

So, I questioned him, "What is your field or profession?"

"Psychopharmacology," he answered. "The study of the effect drugs have on the human mind."

He had been a teacher at a medical school in Portland. No doubt now retired. But ever so alive!

We remained spell-bound for half an hour, during which neither Gary nor I spoke more than two or three sentences. It was as if we had nothing to say of importance in the light of what was pouring out of this man's copious heart.

As we parted, we spontaneously hugged the "stranger." Throughout the day Gary and I returned to his words, knowing that God had touched us powerfully through them. It was fun to muse inwardly of how this guy could possibly have been an angel sent to us on the trail. Yet, surely it is even more spectacular that God could use one human being to touch and bless the lives of two others, who are absolute strangers, so soundly in such a short span of time. That *was* the "miracle."

It was another little miracle was that we gave him "the time of day"—and— that he had stopped us and asked for it!

We pondered a lot that day. We could see how all of us on earth can be a blessing to others when we speak what is on our hearts. It takes being willing to "stick our necks out," rather than to live encased within ourselves, honed in on our "immediates."

It does take time to perchance enrich another, even if briefly. And, it takes daring to see God in all those we meet, realizing these moments as "Divine Appointments." How different would life be, if only we could ride the waves of life experiencing more serendipitous moments!

Solomon's words says it best, "A merry heart does good, like medicine, (Proverbs 17:22).

Think of life as "riding the waves," experiencing the "fun" in the midst of our "functions." Laughter is a major pleasure that we can enjoy daily right at home, relieving much of our pent up tensions. Watch for it, as opportunities abound.

Here's one that occurred while working on a column for Today's News-Herald: I intended to write, "Have you noticed how good it feels to sing, whistle, hum and enjoy music?" However, I inadvertently left the "g" off "sing." When Gary, my excellent, first-line editor, caught this faux pas we laughed—big time! The "g" was quickly added, able to correctly read "sing" instead of "sin." That was close.

We are funny little creatures. Humans. Laughing at ourselves helps us stay sane! It is like medicine to our soul . . . helping us surf through life with excitement!

Prayer—a wondrous mystery

While attempting to learn more about prayer, I have made a concerted effort to draw from others their perceptions of prayer. I am receiving three types of comments: 1) those claiming prayer to be a challenging, yet a rewarding experience; 2) those stating prayer to be too intimate a subject for discussing with others; and 3) those indicating frustrations with prayer.

As regards the last two categories, three people whom I know well, felt free to tell exactly how they felt. One said, "I'm afraid to get very involved with God." The second friend said, "God doesn't answer my prayers. So why should I pray?"

The third said, "I pray, but I don't listen for God to answer back. He might ask something or me that I'm not ready to do."

Apparently a great number of people are either frustrated with prayer or have some fear about giving much of themselves to it.

Stop for a moment and ask yourself, is my prayer life as rewarding as I want it to be? Perhaps your answer is "yes." If so, I admire you. Personally, I spent a lot of my life during which prayer presented a dichotomy. On the one hand it brought hope, strength, peace and an awesome awareness of being loved. But on the other hand the mere thought of the word could bring frustration, guilt, anger and even fear.

Frustration came with feeling like a simpleton when trying to express myself to a holy, awesome God. It was also frustrating to attempt stilling an active mind—one so undisciplined that in a split second it could be off playing "hop-scotch" with memories, or tomorrow's plans.

Guilt came when I didn't take time for prayer. Many days started like a shot out of a cannon and moved swiftly forward before landing with a thud on my pillow 12-14 hours later. On those days good resolutions ducked for cover and popped up later, blanketed with guilt.

Anger came at the thought of communicating with God at times when I was derailed by mistakes or needled with imperfections. Pride wanted perfection. And pride when wounded causes havoc.

At times, there was anger in thinking God had failed to hear my prayers. I slammed shut my window to heaven with questions like: "Why didn't He save that young mother's life so she could nurture and cherish her children? Why does that father, depressed from walking the streets looking for work, have to carry all that pain in his eyes?" Free will, yes, free will. But I would cry nonetheless, "God, isn't there something more you can do?"

Upon truly listening, I could hear Him answer: "There is something *you* can do." Then, I knew what that "something" was. I could at least pray . . . and in some instances see "there is more." Prayer is all about loving and listening . . . coming to comprehend more about God, self and others.

Perhaps that is another reason why prayer was so frustrating. God often offered challenges, and He has been known to require sacrifice. My first inclinations are to escape sacrificing myself, my plans. Yet, on those occasions when obedience rules, indescribable joy follows. A joy that only comes through knowing this sin-prone human heart has linked for a moment with a holy, limitless, loving God. Time to rejoice! We are not alone, here!

Little by little the guilt, the frustration, the anger, and fear are being absorbed as I step through that open door and find the power of love filling me as I have come to trust His acceptance of me . . . as the fires of life serve to strengthen and refine. The trust factor now escalates, putting the questions and insecurities to rest.

As with the finding of any treasure, a price has to be paid. It takes a healthy slice of time each day to produce the spiritual girth that empowers us to resist what our fleshly desires so often pull us toward. After the Holy Spirit is allowed to nourish, enrich and transform, His wisdom can be planted in a fallow, fertile heart.

The mind will always fight the discipline of being quiet, waiting and giving up control. But on those occasions when the will yields, the soul takes flight like a homing pigeon and finds itself at home in the heart of God. When this happens, words do, at times, become a hindrance.

Prayer can be about our needs and our desires. At times it is praise and thanksgiving. Other times, it is intercessions for others. And, majorly, prayer results in action.

Ultimately, prayer is that wondrous mystery of communing with our Maker. It is restorative and restful, like coming home to rest after a trying, tiring day.

A lesson from the Master of Arts

Summer camp—is it just for kids? I don't think so. The question is raised, here, to present what could be a desirable option in planning your own special retreat.

One summer Gary drove me to the Christian Renewal Center near Silverton, Oregon, to a family camp. After staying a couple of days to see me situated, he drove on home to tend to business.

It did not take long to discover a built-in test of stamina. The building I was scheduled to stay in was at the tippy-top of a mountain. It was rightly named Hilltop Lodge. Thank God, it was only a short distance from the chapel. On my way up I could stop for some moments at the altar before continuing toward the summit.

The week brought numerous cherished memories, but the one I recall today is a lesson brought home through craft class. Offerings included painting (with oils and other mediums), calligraphy on Plexiglas, and sandblast woodcraft.

I went for the latter hoping to make something beautiful, yet small and easy. The aging process keeps me mindful of the KISS principle: "Keep it simple stupid." After living many years with a closet full of unfinished projects . . . half-finished sweaters, dried up bottles of paint, expensive X-Acto knives still sharp from lack of use, "I knew "full well" my proficiency level!

Looking around at the "models" on display, I chose a small wood-work with the word "joy." Its simple elegance was intriguing. But while choosing a piece of wood the teacher intervened. She took the plain, smooth board from my hand replacing it with a slab of pine—but, one with a knothole. Against my objections, she said, "Just trust me."

Pushing aside the feeling of being cheated, I took the board, applied the rubber shield, stenciled, then cut my "word" upon it and left. Two days later we were to return to give our work a finishing coat. The actual sandblasting was to be done by the teacher, Carol Cotton. While other participants struggled with intricate patterns on much larger boards, I trudged up to Hilltop to take a rest.

On the third day I went back to crafts. Behold, my art! Transformed by the master-craftsman's hand, it was unrecognizable. And the most intriguing focal point was what had been seen as a blemish—the knothole. Outstanding in its statement, looking somewhat like a tear or a candle's flame, and beside it the simple word, "Joy."

In my hands it seemed to represent life—the hardships, the failures, the detours of plotted goals. From our viewpoint all these seem to devaluate our "wood," meaning our personhood, making it less than the best. Yet, by letting the Master of all arts put these to the test, when the pressure and heat are allowed, the fruit of patience does its work. What looks like sorrows to be avoided or denied come forth transformed by the single advantage of time.

Meanwhile, through perseverance, applying the truths of scripture and persistently covering them with the shield of prayer, we chisel out the statement we want our "finished product" to read—*love, faith, hope, joy*. Simple, yes. Yet, each an elegant symbol time and trust alone can perform.

Then we trust and wait. The "sandblasts of life" come in day-tight increments. Seemingly, rough treatment at times, yet not more than we can bear.

When the Lord Jesus comes for us that finished work will be revealed—no doubt unrecognizable, at first. Yet, there it will be: the personal message our lives have borne. And we will rejoice, owning it all, even the knotholes, each mar and every scar. All transformed. Sins forgiven (those we struggle so hard to forgive ourselves for) will be nowhere in sight. It is the Lord alone who can vanquish them.

Christ at work on the human heart, sees His inspirited dream—even before it is a reality. With preconceived vision, he has faith in us. In allowing the heat and pressure of life on earth, He knows what is being formed . . . a beauteous piece of art. The hand of the Master is upon us. Our part is to submit ourselves." Then, we with Him are co-creators.

Does this not lift our spirits? "God created man in His *own* image; in the image of God He created him; male and female He created them, (Genesis 1:27).

Old challenges seen afresh

Years back our then bachelor son, Tim, "lost his heart" to a lovely, young woman. He was inspired, yet, distraught as her job found his friend moving to another state. However, Tim seemed tireless, able to make a "short distance" out of the 450 miles it took to visit her.

Once, during an hour together before his leave-taking he and I talked and prayed. Upon telling him of something I planned to do for his friend, Tim's eyes filled with love and he said, "Oh, Mom … if you do that for her it will be as if you are doing it for me."

A momentary sense of *déjà vu* hit me. I recalled Jesus spoke these same words to His disciples while teaching them about the final judgement. Using the parable of Matthew 25:31-40. He said, "And, the King will answer and say to them, 'Assuredly, I say to you, in as much as you did *it* to one of the least of these My brethren, you did *it* unto me."

When Tim made this point on behalf of the one he loved his words were rich with meaning. I thought of Jesus and how when we serve others, surely it is as if we have done it *unto Him.*

Perhaps occasionally it is important to examine "heart motives." Is the service we are giving to our fellow man really an act of love? Done with love of our Lord? Or, out of our hopes to please, gain favor or be noticed? Prestige? A place in the "inner circle"? Power?

How often are deeds done out of a sense of obligation—working to pay back what we have received? The truth is we don't have to prove our worth or *earn our space*! God created us. We are His children—good, acceptable and beloved. On the other hand, pride is, at times, a motivator. Pride can come through our *always* being the one who helps. Always *needing* to be *the giver*. Sometimes it is good and right to sit back, allowing others opportunity to serve. It is very important to also be the *receiver of loving care.*

There are times when we serve others out of sympathy. Even though this emotion is a valid response, we best be careful. Here again there can be a self-serving twist. Conrad Baars, MD wrote in *Healing the Unaffirmed,* that the emphasis must lie "on a state of being for and with another, of being moved inwardly by his goodness and unique worth prior to doing anything for him." Now, that's the ultimate as regards being with others.

There are also times, out of fear of disappointing another or losing face, we give. But, when we look at the life of our Master we see that of all the things He could have done, He moved and acted only through the motivation of love. In His Words, "I do only what I see the Father doing." And His Father, after all, was love. 1 John 4:8, assures us God is love.

Now let's take a moment to look at what, for many of us, is a common failure: the inability to accept and lovingly serve our own selves. Dr. Carl Jung put it eloquently: "what if I should discover that the least of all brethren, the poorest of all beggars, the most insolent of all offenders, yes, even the very enemy himself – that these live within me; that I myself stand in need of the alms of my own kindness, that I am to myself the enemy who is to be loved?" Jung was concerned about our refusing to receive the least among the lowly *in ourselves* with open arms."

We esteem our bodies enough to shave and bathe, groom and consume nourishing foods, yet whip the inner self into frenzies of *doing* as we have not yet discovered the beauty of being. Once we are able to cherish the true essence of ourselves and what we were created to be, that which is done to validate and love ourselves will act as spring boards moving us speedily and spontaneously into God-directed service. New fervor and vision will be held.

Could it be possible Jesus wore a smile when He said: "Love the Lord your God with all your heart, all your mind and all your soul. And love your neighbor as yourself"? Was He gently using humor to make His point of how far we are from loving God until we can also love *ourselves*—then our neighbors?

Let us not mistake hedonism; pervasive consumerism; demanding or expecting allegiance from others—outright selfishness for the act of validly loving one's self. Truly knowing how to generously treat the person called "me" *to the best I can offer* is an artful way to live.

In this "heart-oriented" place, we can break forth into joy, giving thanksgiving for the beauty of our personhood." And, in so doing heap love and delight upon our Lord.

Trusting the Father

We parent's do have our memories, many of which are beyond the wealth of gold. They keep blessing us as we think of them. I recall today one of our three sons, at age four, asking if he could go down to the ditch to float his boats. I told him "no." His older brother was not there to go with him, and I could not.

He looked up. With eyes filling with tears and a quivering lip he said, "Mamma, you have a horn on your heart!"

I swept him up in my arms, danced him around with laughter and we both were touched by love. That was a lot of years back. Today this son has children of his own and fully understands why at times I told him "no."

This is the way it is between us and God. We cannot know or understand His ways. He is so much more knowledgeable than we can be. Apostle Paul described looking at our "todays" with all that is happening in the here and now. He said, "For now we see in a mirror, dimly, but then face to face. Now I know in part, but then I shall know just as I also am known," (1 Corinthians 13:12).

Have you had the experience of asking God for something you felt must happen? Then, deciding after waiting and waiting that He must be saying "no?"

God always answers. It is either "yes," "no," or "wait"—not a verbal answer, for the way we learn to hear Him speak into our lives comes by faith. With time and experience, we learn to trust. God does know best.

How tragic life would be if God were to say "yes," just to please us—to guarantee our friendship. Imagine Him granting that which could work against our happiness? A coddling, permissive God would offer no stability, no order and no safety.

Many billions of people have placed their trust in God throughout the history of time. Those who write about it say the same thing in different words: peace, love and joy result from this trust. In fact the peace that comes "surpasses all understanding," (Philippians 4:6-7). Also, within this trust comes the knowledge that this life here on terra firma is not all that is in store for us—eternity will be our future home.

God wants us to put our trust in Him, while also knowing sometimes what we ask for in life is not granted. Yet, peace comes in knowing God is with us and will not leave us to figure out the future on our own. Asking for daily guidance is one of the greatest of all prayers.

It does take trust to turn our lives over, making it our habit to be enriched by God's presence, finding inspiring guidance through reading about His will within Holy Writ. Yet, it brings riches of heart and soul far beyond any other way of living. Instead of being temporary and deadly, like alcohol or illicit drugs, it is life giving and healing—to say the very least, here.

Ours is a dependable Father who came to us in Christ. One who has set forth some rules. His "yes" is "yes." And his "no," is "no." Yet in His love, He does not force us to obey. Always we have choice.

At times we go our own way. We rebel against God. Wanting our own way, we plunge in head first only to find shallow waters. It is a loving Father who binds our wounds, bidding us to rest while He heals us.

Other times we say we will "live the life of faith," yet our hearts lag far behind. "Lip service," it is called, and hypocrisy. Before long we are tested and the "Pharisee" within comes to light. (A part of us that can act religious, while being self-centered and unloving.) None of us want to own this fellow, "the Pharisee," big as life, at times. What could be less childlike than a pompous Pharisee?

Matthew 18:2-4, illustrates this for us, "Then Jesus called a little child to Him, set him in the midst of them, [3] and said, Assuredly, I say to you, unless you are converted and become as little children, you will by no means enter the kingdom of heaven. Therefore whoever humbles himself as this little child is the greatest in the kingdom of heaven." Childlike. Absolutely honest . . . close abiding . . . dependent on the

Father . . . not hesitating to spill tears of disappointment, frustration, anger. Cleansed of hostility, room is made for Truth. Touched by His love, the "dance" begins. Oh, the joy of growing in trust of the Father—knowing He truly cares. In the midst of all, God understands our needs and is listening to our prayers. Our part is to watch and wait, *trusting*, as He leads us through our difficulties and uncertainties.

Why do we fear becoming childlike? What does it take for us to trust God enough to be so vulnerable, as to depend on Him? Is it possible to be free of all forms of deception, bringing absolute honesty to our relationships? How can one trust so totally after years of being "adult?"

David, king of Israel in Psalm 131:1-2, wrote of his childlike trust, "Lord, my heart is not haughty, nor my eyes lofty. Neither do I concern myself with great matters, nor with things too profound for me. Surely I have calmed and quieted my soul, like a weaned child with his mother; like a weaned child is my soul within me."

Surely we have our moments of perverting the rules, making them mean what we want them to mean . . . times of elevating self, becoming "the know-it-all." But, oh, the pain we can spare ourselves by trusting the Father, following His ways . . . becoming the trusting child.

Perhaps the greatest challenge of all in life is that of developing as a human to the point of "walking and talking" with the Father. Impossible? We know of one man who is recorded in Scripture as having achieved this. But how many know this is an option for us? Even so, how many would desire it? Enoch did. (See Genesis 5:24). Could it be that God saw this man had reached completion—so He took him home? Even a sincere effort in attempting to live such a life opens the way to the truest and fullest exercise in faith. This is a "walk" in which we can know we are never alone . . . and always loved.

The 'setting' of the soul

A showcase of opals lay before my eyes—any one of them could be mine. My father stood watching as I studied them.

After Dad retired, he learned through a lapidary shop in Phoenix how to cut and set stones. And, here was Dad's treasure stash, fresh work of his hands, yes, but mostly from his heart.

Patiently, he waited as I placed each one on my ring finger before making a decision. It was fun, but serious. Saying "yes" to one excluded all the others.

This morning I looked again at his gift and thought of how much his work with stones is like a writer's work with words. Words, those ever present entities found kicking along life's path. Writers pick over and sort through them, and place them in the tumbler of our hearts. Next, we cut and buff, examine and plan, finally setting them in sentences and paragraphs.

Then, when they are shining as best we can make them, we place our offerings in "showcases"—reverently for readers. Our gift. Some will be liked and some won't, holding power to evoke great emotion, or to get us stoned— these wondrous things called words.

After meditating on these thoughts this morning, I opened my Bible, which has become a treasured way to start my day. Romans 3: 23-24, touches me afresh, "For all have sinned and fall short of the glory of God, being justified freely by His grace through the redemption that is in Christ Jesus . . . (Yeah! He is at work in me!)

The dictionary shows two applicable meanings for "justified," 1) "to pronounce free from guilt or blame, and 2) to adjust or arrange exactly." How clear, the likeness between us and the stones beneath our feet. We, also were covered by "dirt." Spotted by God. Picked up and chosen. Incubated in His heart. Now in process—being cut and buffeted as we bounce about upon each other within daily life God's jewels in formation. Sure, a long ways from completion, but coming along according to His design.

Thinking of better times

Everybody knows you can't pick a handful of huckleberries in less than a second. Right? Wrong….

My husband, Gary, and I spent a lazy week in McCall, Idaho, one summer. There in that beautiful, restful setting the one hint of ambition I had was spent in a couple of hours of "huckleberrying" (a verb long known to natives). The berries were sparse and tiny. Heaven only knows why we didn't give up earlier. But I kept telling myself, each one of these little suckers is a tiny burst of flavor—it won't take many to make tomorrow's pancakes a memorable taste treat.

By the time we had picked for two hours my back was talking, mosquito bites itching and I was begging to quit. Gary's reply trailed in from the distance, "I'll be finished with this patch in a minute."

I had visions of plunging into the lake; his visions were of a pie. Now, a pie takes at least four cups of berries, not to mention considerable work and firing up the wood-burning oven in a rustic lakeside cabin. This was my vacation, after all.

Picking baby berries can get dull, causing the mind to wander. In the quiet beauty of the woods it wasn't long before I was thinking of God's great extravaganza. Pockets of water cradled in mountains high, standing at wait for seekers of rest and recreation; meadows of wildflowers looking like crowds dressed in violet, yellow and blue; stately pines responding to the whispers of a caressing breeze.

God spared no effort with His creations, right down to the little huckleberry waiting to be plucked—tiny, easy to overlook. Yet, each holds a savory moment of yum.

There seems to be a parallel here. With close to 7.8 billion human beings on the earth it seems incredible that the individual has importance. But like the little huckleberry, each has flavor. Some are bitter; some are sweet; some sour and some salty.

Salty! Wasn't that what Jesus called his followers? A common substance, often taken for granted, yet invaluable when used to preserve, purify and season. Jesus is wanting that for us. And, ***really*** . . . is that true of us?

How sweet it would have been if the Lord had said, "You're my little huckleberries." But he didn't. He said, "You are the salt of the earth." Salt. It almost takes a grimace to say the word. And—whoa! He continues, saying, "But if the salt loses its flavor, how shall it be seasoned? It is then good for nothing but to be thrown out and trampled underfoot by men," (Matthew 5:13).

Sometimes we don't act like salt, but more like the huckleberry—an exotic little temptress or tempter, easily crushed, staining and tainting, and capable of drawing a lot of attention to itself.

On the other hand, how challenging it is to be salt. A preserving, refining, flavorful agent in our own little corner of the world.

Meanwhile, back at McCall. Finished with berry picking and headed for "home's" front door, I hear Gary yell, "Hey, you!"

I turn in time to see a little guy not more than two feet tall making away with a fist full of huckleberries. He had reached deep into Gary's bucket. Berries tumbled through his little fingers, falling all around his feet.

"Do you know it took hours to pick those?" Gary squalled.

The child looks up with innocence as he hurriedly pokes more berries into his "pie hole."

Laughter did follow our shock, but inwardly we begrudged Todd, our youngest son, every berry.

A handful of huckleberries in less than a second? Yes, it is possible. But only if you are a sneaky little snitch lying in wait for a weary-eyed, plodding plucker headed to the lakeside cabin . . . with visions of huckleberries—albeit a cup shy of a full pie.

Can we have peace?

Most of us have joked about the ostrich which allegedly sticks its head in the sand to hide from danger.

Goggling reveals the truth: "As flightless birds, ostriches are unable to build nests in trees, so they lay their eggs in holes dug in the ground. To make sure that the eggs are evenly heated, they occasionally stick their heads into the nest to rotate the eggs, which makes it look like they're trying to hide—hence the myth."

Nature often teaches. Yet, the legend of the ostrich to, "Bury one's head in the sand when danger is near" is of no help. However, the true lesson of the ostrich is portrayed well: "Find what meets your needs and use it to your best advantage."

Ostriches don't have our highly developed brains, but their instincts amaze us. We humans, on the other hand have vast amounts of knowledge, yet we find it hard to live in peace. A factor that best helps us gain peace is the truth that we are not alone here on terra firma. God is with us and we have a grand and mighty connection with Him through prayer.

It is with prayer that *we* have a peace that may seem incomprehensible while so many dangers lie far and wide. This peace is experienced and enjoyed for people who know how to "plug in." For Christians, this comes through dedicating our lives to the amazing truths found in Scripture. Proverbs 3:5-6, reveals our steadfast hinge, "Trust in the Lord with all your heart, and lean not on your own understanding; in all your ways acknowledge Him, and He shall direct your paths." This is a "peace-maker." And, it works.

Many scripture passages bring peace to the soul through helping us let go our worries, our fears. Like, "Be anxious for nothing, but in everything by prayer and supplication, with thanksgiving, let your requests be made known to God; and the peace of God, which surpasses all understanding, will guard your hearts and minds through Christ Jesus," (Philippians 4:6-7).

It is impossible to have peace of heart if, like the proverbial ostrich, we bury our hearts in the sands of ignorance, fear and confusion. Doing so serves to create anxiety and inertia. Yet, we do hear the news or read it in print. I heard the good advice of a psychologist speaking at a medical center in Scottsdale years ago. He said, "Cut your news watching by 80% for good mental health." This advice applies even more so today.

"What does God want of us?" There is no question that God wants us to have peace. After His resurrection, Jesus found His disciplines in a state far from peace. The crucifixion blew their minds! They were afraid and hiding. Jesus said, "Peace be with you, as the Father has sent me, so I send you." Then he breathed on them, saying, "Receive the Holy Spirit," (John 20: 21-13).

God wants us to receive His Holy Spirit. Why? Because it brings us a peace that empowers us. Having the Holy Spirit empowers us to forgive those who have hurt us in life . . . and to forgive some hard things we have to endure. Peace brings courage—a courage that empowers us to follow our hearts.

If the desires of our hearts are wholesome, it is the Spirit of God within that helps us achieve them. At times this may find us speaking up about issues, pitting our wits against the "wind" of what can cause havoc in our lives, in our community, or in the world at large.

Just recently, many participated in peaceful protests against current wrongs that break hearts and ruins lives—even takes lives. Unfortunately, some protests were not-so-peaceful. God will never put it in our hearts to hurt innocent people or put them, or their property, in harm's way.

Interestingly enough, although Jesus promised personal peace that comes as we follow His teachings, He did not promise world peace. A larger plan was laid in place for that, which is not the topic here.

We live in a warring world. An imperfect world. Yet, it is where we learn to be strong and we learn to love in the midst of all that comes our way.

To have personal peace in the midst of it all is to read the Bible and simply do what it says.

God, a commander—or, a loving Father?

No ocean vacations this year. Today, it takes visiting past memories to recall standing at the ocean's edge watching the sun give its evening salute. One evening comes to mind most easily. We were at Cannon Beach, Oregon. Each night of our vacation Gary and I made a beach trek from Tolovana Inn to Haystack Rock knowing this was the spot to be at day's end.

But this night was different. A Coast Guard helicopter hovered overhead. An ambulance stood at the shore along with the sheriff of Cannon Beach and several hundred people. A few hours before a young woman had been rescued from beyond the surf. The man she was with had not been found.

The atmosphere was charged with dread and apprehension. A mother, seeing her child approach the seas, ran forward shouting "Get away from the water!" Sand castles stood deserted.

The 23-year-old man's body, although spotted at one time by air, was not found. Two days later the young man was listed as "missing and presumed drowned."

While talking with the sheriff on the night of the drowning he said, "It happens every year. People just won't respect the ocean."

I think of life and how little respect we give it. Thinking it will always be there for us, bringing beauty and pleasure, we forget its supreme function. Life, like the sea, is continually moving, daily depositing new treasures at our feet. With the power of such motion comes ever present dangers.

Life, like the sea, is continually moving, daily depositing new treasures at our feet. With the power of such motion comes ever present dangers. Having a tendency to block that truth from our minds, we expect only good to come our way. Then, when tragedy strikes we cry, "Why? How could life play such a dirty trick?"

Unfortunately, we often place ourselves in jeopardy. We go "beyond the surf." Foolishly, we forget the rules or guidelines. How often do we look at the ways in which we have ignored the Ten Commandments, and ultimately Jesus' commandment, which He called *the greatest of all*—that of letting love of God, self and others rule our lives?

Ours is a time when many give little thought, if any to God's commandments. Seeing Him as a Commander instead of a loving Father, a different way is sought. When in truth, more than any earthly father, He treasures the life we breathe … our joy … our laughter, and gave rules seeking to protect us.

Living on earth involves risk; sometimes sorrow comes when we have taken every precaution. Then our Father is there to comfort and help us find meaning in the midst of the pain. But much of our personal sorrow comes directly from choosing situation ethics or the philosophy "if it isn't hurting anyone, why not?" Overlooking the Father's rules.

What a precarious choice—much like pitting one's strength against the ocean's surf, saying, "I'll take my chances."

A short time before Jesus was crucified He stood looking over what we call "The Holy City" and cried out, "Oh Jerusalem, Jerusalem . . . How often I wanted to gather your children together the way a hen gathers her chicks under her wings, but you were unwilling," (Matthew 23:26).

Centuries come and centuries go. But there does not seem to be much change in the human heart. We still so often desire to go our own way that seems pleasurable and self-satisfying . . . yet, deplore the price of our self-destruction.

Can you relate?

An exasperating experience happened last week while working with an offshore tech about a software problem. Upon calling for help, the cue was looping; I couldn't get a person. Then upon reaching one, he could not find my account. Forty-five minutes had passed!

People talk about losing their religion. "Rankled, in the moment, I lost my perspective. Words like "d_ _ and h_ _ _," were trying to surface. Yikes! I never swear! Now, my temper became the bigger concern. When I asked the Lord, "Help me understand what is behind this anger," then an old, painful memory arose. Funny how early-life happenings can come vividly alive affecting a current situation.

It is important to follow the advice I so frequently give to others: "Honor your emotions and identify old messages derived from wounds of the past—that can still affect your life." Yes. There it was. The old memory had engrained a message. And, it was that message while working with the off-shore tech that forcefully came alive, "They didn't care enough!" So, I am back to the drawing board for more inner work.

Once we get a taste of the freedom that comes with healing our emotional wounds, we are more inclined to invest time for dealing with difficult emotions and forgiving the past. Joy springs up from the soul as a result.

The truth is this: We can't reach our max in wholeness by putting a lid on our difficult feelings. Why? Because doing so also finds us capping off most of our joy as well. Ideally, we reckon with feelings that are difficult to handle, versus pushing those down deep inside. What a great pleasure it is to work through the pain and begin to praise God for all the goodness in our lives. Soon, more and more excitement, enthusiasm, gladness, and peace of heart are present. These are the keys to living a life of emotional freedom. We can live on "the celebration side." ***Voile!***

Through the ages, wisdom has flowed within humanity. Socrates once said, "Know thyself." He knew well that "the life which is unexamined is not worth living." Then, William Shakespeare wrote, "To thine own self be true." These writers urge us to examine our hearts. King David's words, after he looked within, are common to my own. He cried out, "Create in me a clean heart, O God, and renew a steadfast spirit within me," (Psalm 51:10). The greatest of all wisdom comes to play when, after examining, we align our lives with what God wants of us. With God's help, our hearts are made clean, and we are back on the "solid ground" of righteous living wherein we respect ourselves, enjoy others, and abide within God's intentions.

If we, as believers, can't rejoice, but instead live and act as if life on earth is a trial to be endured—we are not living in truth. This world is only a brief part of eternal existence. Actually, we are just passing through. Life here, presents us with an opportunity to learn how to become more and more deeply involved with the Lord, our Creator. It is within this wonderful privilege that we hear God's call and find how best we can develop our gifts and meaningfully serve the needs of our families and others.

Jesus talked much about joy, even as He neared the shadow of the cross. And, for sure, there is joy in the presence of the Lord. We can feel that joy and that Presence while reading Scripture. Within those pages, the character and wondrous nature of God shows up. We see that our Creator wants the best for us. ***We are meant to enjoy our lives*** and this beautiful earth.

Joy comes when we capture some of the essence of what God and His goodness is about. The Bible says, "Rejoice in the Lord always. Again I will say, rejoice! Let your gentleness be known to all men. The Lord is at hand. Do not be anxious for nothing, but in everything by prayer and supplication, with thanksgiving, let your requests be known to God; and the peace of God, which surpasses all understanding, will guard your hearts and minds through Christ Jesus. Finally, brethren, whatever things are true, whatever things are noble, whatever things are just, whatever things are pure, whatever things are lovely, whatever things are of good report, if there is any virtue and if there is anything praiseworthy—meditate on these things," (Philippians 4:4-8).

Contrary to what some people believe regarding a Christian's life, God doesn't limit our potential and possibilities. Rather, God vastly expands them.

A medley of truth for troubled hearts

Difficult times come to all of us. Notice how differently you feel after reading the short passages I have typed below. It is like entering a "different space." There is a reason for that.

God can lift and comfort us. If you find yourself in a difficult space in life, see the difference it can make to read these passages:

John 14:1-3 – "Let not your heart be troubled; you believe in God, believe also in Me. In My Father's house are many mansions; if it were not so, I would have told you. I go to prepare a place for you. And if I go and prepare a place for you, I will come again and receive you to Myself; that where I am, there you may be also,"

Matthew 11:28-30 – "Come to Me, all you who labor and are heavy laden, and I will give you rest. Take My yoke upon you, and learn from Me, for I am gentle and lowly in heart, and you will find rest for your souls. For My yoke is easy and My burden is light."

Isaiah 1:18-19 –"'Come now, let us reason together, 'says the LORD, 'though your sins are like scarlet, they shall be as white as snow; though they are red like crimson, they shall be as wool. If you are willing and obedient, you shall eat the good of the land; but if you refuse and rebel . . ." [well, let's just say "things won't go so well.]

Psalm 23: 1-6 – "The Lord *is* my shepherd; I shall not want. He makes me to lie down in green pastures; He leads me beside the still waters. He restores my soul; He leads me in the paths of righteousness for His name's sake. Yea, though I walk through the valley of the shadow of death, I will fear no evil; for You *are* with me; Your rod and Your staff, they comfort me. You prepare a table before me in the presence of my enemies; You anoint my head with oil; my cup runs over. Surely goodness and mercy shall follow me all the days of my life; and I will dwell in the house of the Lord forever."

Revelations 3:20 –"Behold, I stand at the door and knock. If anyone hears My voice and opens the door, I will come in to him and dine with him, and he with Me."

John 3:16-17 – "For God so loved the world that he gave His only Son so that everyone who believes in Him may not perish but may have eternal life. For God did not send His Son into the world to condemn the world, but that the world through Him might be saved."

Isaiah 26:3 – "You will keep him in perfect peace, whose mind is stayed on you, because he trusts in you. Trust in the Lord forever, for in YAH, the Lord, is everlasting strength."

2 Timothy 1:7 – "For God has not given us a spirit of fear, but of power and of love and of a sound mind."

Jeremiah 29:11-14 – "For I know the thoughts that I think toward you, says the LORD, thoughts of peace and not of evil, to give you a future and a hope. Then you will call upon Me and go and pray to Me, and I will listen to you. And you will seek Me and find *Me,* when you search for Me with all your heart. I will be found by you, says the LORD, and I will bring you back from your captivity . . ."

Psalm 91:1-2 – "He who dwells in the secret place of the Most High shall abide under the shadow of the Almighty. I will say of the LORD, '"He is my refuge and my fortress; My God, in Him I will trust.'"

Psalm 1:1 – "Blessed is the man who walks not in the counsel of the ungodly, nor stands in the path of sinners, nor sits in the seat of the scornful; but his delight is in the law of the LORD, and in His law he meditates day and night."

Romans 8:1 – "There is therefore now no condemnation to those who are in Christ Jesus, who do not walk according to the flesh, but according to the Spirit!"

Romans 8:28 – "And we know that all things work together for good to those who love God, to those who are the called according to *His* purpose."

Psalm 37:4 – "Delight yourself also in the LORD, and He shall give you the desires of your heart."

If alarmed or unsure—having difficult thoughts—call a pastor, priest or rabbi. These leaders can help you. Or, call a trusted friend who also prays. God our Creator is with us and He alone can heal our souls, quieting our concerns and fears. God made us and has a plan for our lives.

Birthdays—who needs them?

A birthday is coming! And, the numbers are getting larger! I have no shame, only gladness in having survived so long in such a challenging place as planet earth!

Friends are a wonderful part of life. I recall a birthday spent with a friend whose front door was about 25 miles from my own. We laughed, exchanged gifts and told stories, as her birthday is only ten days from mine. Given a few moments alone, I wander out on her deck where the view is grand. Crowned with sunshine, all of nature seems to shout, "Celebrate!"

Vines wind their way along the deck, carrying the tiniest grapes ever seen. Bending low, I peer close to examine such a find as fruit in embryotic state. They look like little mustard seeds, only green, hanging by a thread of a stem.

Tempted, I nearly pull off a cluster in order to better see, yet a stronger urge says, "Stop! Think of the wine that will not be!" Yes, even this minute offering holds potential for moments of joy to be savored by some soul. The urge to pluck it loose for curious pleasure is gone as I realize my innate tendencies to serve and satisfy self as if in neon lights.

Here on my birthday, the celebration is suddenly ditched as thoughts of abortion crowd in. How disquieting! Whatever your viewpoint, we are all affected. It is important to keep thinking about this—and to continue speaking our impassioned truth . . . even more so, pondering and listening for God's take on this, through Scripture and through prayer.

Some time back, I, too, was a mere embryo like the grapes now viewed. It was not a good time for my parents to bring a child into the world. My mother told me of sitting by the hours weeping as I lay slumbering within her womb. My gratitude for the gift of life includes thinking of her suffering, plus nearly losing her life through my birth. What if abortion had been legal? Perhaps I would not have come to be here on earth. I would not be sitting, writing to you. There would be no birthdays, here, at least not for me.

Life is a gift that carries God's promise to indwell us, provide for and protect us. With God's help we are up to any and all tasks we are called to face. There is no circumstance too hard for Him to work through and transmute into goodness and glory for those who will trust.

Within each new child gifts await to unfurl and to bloom. Scientists, musicians, writers, teachers—Saints?

The joy that is to flow through a little child cannot be compared with any other gift of life. Besides having Gary to love, my three sons are the best part of my life.

Sometimes the little people who come to us have a very short time to strut their stuff. I think of Matthew, a three-year-old who died close to my birthday in the past. Residing in Washington State with his parents, he was not someone I met and knew. He was the nephew of friends. Through them I knew of this little one's journey. Many of us prayed, hoping for his healing as he suffered immensely for the entire duration of his short life. But he came gifted and he gave.

You see, Matthew would not give up. Once having seen the glory of sunshine, he held tenaciously to life. My friend Shirley said of him, "That little guy was something else. A fighter . . . he just had a no-good body." Now released, he has gone to the arms of the Father of all—healed, but not without first fulfilling his destiny. His legacy rests within the family tree—most of all, but also through the strength, courage and unity that came as thousands of believers coast to coast joined them in prayer for Matthew to be able to stay with us.

What about *our* families? So often there is a tendency to simply tolerate those closest to us, valuing more those who live at some distance. Yet, are not our family members given for both finite and infinite purposes? Usually, those who are closest to us have power to rub us in ways that can best polish our rough edges. Rubbing and emotional squeezing happens between us which doesn't always feel good. Still, it brings out the wine: the treasure of our belonging to one another, the history of our love.

With God's grace and His Holy Spirit within, we can transcend the cognitive dissonance that comes with being human having a felt need to control everything . . . our impatience and fears. If we can master these daily foes, we can sip the various "vintages," savoring precious moments with the people God has given to us to love.

Luke 12:6-7 holds an amazing truth, "Are not five sparrows sold for two copper coins? And not one of them is forgotten before God. But the very hairs of your head are all numbered. Do not fear therefore; you are of more value than many sparrows."

May God grant us the grace to let Him carry our fears and apprehensions when we encounter difficulties and experiences that look too difficult. Let's ever look forward to the good that He allows to come to us, along with the strength and empowerment. Through all, we learn to trust. How glorious it is to see how our Creator—Father God, turns to good what looks bad to us.

Happy birthday to each of you, on whatever day of the year you arrived from a womb!

What's in *your* drawers?

This has to be the only time in my history in which every drawer, cabinet and closet is set in order. Now, spiffy clean. In fact, our whole house has received a "going through" as my mother would say. Even the door to the pantry can now be left open without shame or blame. Not a weed grows in our yard and the plants are each trimmed and fertilized. The garage is next. For sure, the pandemic's "at home lock down" order has left us with something for which to be thankful. To some degree, many of us are "spic and span."

Speaking of this, my memory flashed back a few decades to another time of deciding to clean all the drawers in the house. Our three sons were young, having growth spurts and Gary and I were . . . let's just say "not quite prepared" for finding scantily-clad girlie pictures in our 11-year-old's bottom drawer. Putting our heads together, we decided to pin those pictures on all four walls of the kid's bedroom.

He came home from school, went to his room—and did not come out for a very, very long time. We sat at the dinner table calling for him to come join us. Finally, he did. His face was solemn and white as a sheet. He looked—well—a bit stunned.

Needless to say we never saw girlie pictures in our home, again. Fortunately, our son was healthy enough to take this in the stride of life. It could have been different. And, after the fact, as parents know—that was a dumb thing to do to a kid! But, who doesn't do some stupid stuff while raising a family?

What about venturing into our *mental* drawers, meaning those places where we hold beliefs and ideas that no longer serve well? So often these are hidden away and we hardly give them an occasional nod—that is until some phrase or statement pops out of our mouths that reveals them.

Take for instance a statement I heard a person say recently, "What does God have to do with anything?" Well . . . maybe everything. But, none-the-less, that man was entitled to his belief—even to express it, given freedom of speech.

Yet, take *our* beliefs. Most experts agree that by age six, a person's belief system is reasonably well formed. But, it is probably safe to say only a small portion of humanity questions beliefs formed so early in life. Somewhere after mid-life, I "got it." People believe what they want to believe.

It is so uncomfortable to change a belief. People much prefer to leave things "as is" when it comes to long held beliefs. It is easy to get stuck with self-assurances or self-sufficiency that can produce prejudice and pride. Rather than do a little self-scrutinizing about our beliefs, frequently, we excuse ourselves, opting to spew "it's all's good," or some other self-satisfying statement. However, problems come, when our beliefs find us behaving in ways that make us less open and authentic.

What about habits that just can't seem to align themselves with what we know could best fit with having a good life? These seem to have a "drawer" of their own. It's one that gets slammed shut a lot with a mere thought, like, "I'll do something about that tomorrow."

Then there is the resentment drawer. The mere smell of it keeps us from opening that one. Still, we dare not leave it to smolder. I feel sure the Lord would say, "Forgive it. Remember, I have forgiven you."

These are deep places of the soul that deserve some pondering. Scripture says, "For nothing is secret that will not be revealed, nor *anything* hidden that will not be known and come to light," (Luke 8:17).

The Apostle Paul said in 1 Corinthians 4:4-5, "For I know of nothing against myself, yet I am not justified by this; but He who judges me is the Lord. Therefore judge nothing before the time, until the Lord comes, who will both bring to light the hidden things of darkness and reveal the counsels of the hearts. Then each one's praise will come from God."

Most likely, looking at our beliefs and our behaviors—shifting into "clean up" mode when we need to, is a good idea. After all, "to repent" simply means, "to turn around and go in the opposite direction."

Seems we owe it to ourselves to take time periodically to look at matters that are important within the scope of our desire to have a good time with God in heaven for eternity.

What makes a church vital?

Recently, I read the newsletter of a Phoenix pastor that intrigues, plus brings a chuckle. Ken Page of Orangewood Presbyterian Church in Phoenix writes,

"I once asked my Sunday school teacher what heaven would be like, and she replied that 'Heaven will be a lot like church, but it will go on forever!'

That was the day I decided to become a sinner!

Church?!

Forever?!

I was in fifth grade. I liked singing, but wasn't as good with words like Ebenezer and prostrate. Mostly church was just stuff I didn't understand, and an hour was already too long. Forever?!

Over time I began to understand. If she had said that heaven was a lot like Christian camp pool only forever, I would have gotten it immediately. Of course I loved the archery, the silly games, but I also sensed something was different about the people. There was a palpable love at camp. There was way less teasing and bullying and sarcasm, and if an adult was around when these things happened (sometimes I was the perpetrator) they handled it . . . gently. It was almost . . . as if . . . they valued us . . . even the fifth grade boys!

A few years later, I would have gotten it if she'd said heaven is like youth group only forever. Youth group was awesome—again, silly games and pizza. But there was also something different about youth group. My gifts were valued there, and my faults were tolerated and nudged toward better behavior. My school friends were into bad things. My youth group friends weren't. They actually had two groups of friends, too, but we didn't have to fit in with the crowd when we were with each other. We shaped each other's lives for the better!

My senior year in high school, I actually would have gotten it if the teacher had said "heaven is like Sunday school, only forever." That was the year that a close friend of mine died on a Saturday night. I found out in Sunday school. I burst into tears and ran from the room crying. Back in the 1900's men didn't cry in front of others. As soon as I got into the parking lot, I realized that I didn't actually want to be alone. No sooner did I turn around than I found that my whole class had followed me into the parking lot and we cried and prayed together, and we did it for LONGER THAN AN HOUR!

Heaven is like the very best parts of church, only forever! Church should be a taste of heaven that one day we will have forever! Yeah! I get it!"

Thank you, Pastor Ken!

There are some essentials for any church that intends to effectively portray the love Jesus Christ has given to us . . . and hopes to effectively extend it to others. These non-negotiables have transcended time and culture:

1) Every church should uphold the gospel—the good news of Christ; 2) every church should teach God's Word as its ultimate authority; 3) music is a must, as it helps a soul transcend the pressures of "last week;" 4) prayerful leadership and people able and willing to share their "quest for heaven"; 5) *o*pportunities to read the Bible together and study it as to how it pertains to our daily lives, and 6) congregational, prayerful worship; and 7) Sunday school.

The last entry is extra important, as it makes a huge difference in a person's life to grow up enjoying Sunday school. Never is Sunday school boring, as adults called to this ministry make it fun.

Ultimately, church is for worshiping God together in community. It is also a place where people can go to be renewed in spirit. It is a place to find truth. But, the best of all churches is where love is present and new comers are enjoyed.

People want to return when they feel cared about and welcomed to return. A copy of the church's mission is the best gift to hand to them, along with the phone number of the pastor and the number of one additional person (like a deacon, or elder) who can be called to pray, answer questions, or assist in times of trouble.

Of course, no one is looking for perfection, right? For, while here on earth, there are no perfect people. We are a forgiven people!

Why does God need praise?

Talk about praising God doesn't take place much. In fact it can be a little frightening to some. Visions of fanaticism come to mind. People shouting "Praise the Lord," and "Hallelujah" can be unsettling for some. Although, praise to God is rightfully vocalized, it more often exudes gently as we inwardly worship during our prayer times. It also arises as an inner rejoicing that is felt, at points, when we are captured by the beauty of nature. A sunset, for instance. Loving thoughts of our Creator exacts praise from the heart.

On the other hand, let's not forget ancient Israel's King David. There was something wondrous going on between him and God. His praise was vocal, and it was copious. The validity of David's praise and adoration is seen in the power that flowed from his life. God was obviously with him.

King David celebrated life. 2 Samuel 6:14-16, shows him dancing in reckless abandon as he praised God. Michal, his wife, scorned and despised him for this. He was not even fully clothed, after all. Yet, while she lived out her days as a barren, bitter woman, he went down in history in glory.

As Pierre Teilhard de Chardin, put it, "Joy is the infallible sign of the presence of God."

It is interesting how differently God makes His people. Like light bulbs, some have greater capacity for wattage. It is true, too, that some receive a surge of power, cast a great beam, then blow out quickly. Others exude a bright, long lasting steady light, while many gently burn like a soft flame with a low glow with no noticeable variance. And God needs us all. He does not have favorites. The secret is to seek through our spiritual practices to be filled with as much light as we are capable of bearing. For, clearly, it is light that vanquishes darkness.

How do we get the utmost measure of light? I believe it is through praise.

The word “praise” appears 306 times throughout Scripture, 134 of which are direct requests to do it. Why? Because God inhabits (dwells in) the praise of His people, (Psalm 22:3). It seems the light of Christ expands in us as we speak gratitude for God’s goodness in our lives.

If multitudes of angels stand before the throne praising God constantly, surely it has great worth. Through it we enter into union with Him, connecting with the powerful, loving presence as our God. Through offering praise and gratitude, we are uplifted, able to transcend the hardest of all disappointments and difficulties of life.

David, who seemed far ahead of most humans in understanding eternal truths, proclaimed, “I will bless the LORD at all times; His praise shall continually be in my mouth, (Psalm 34:1).” In the New Testament, Paul was the most outstanding “voice” teaching the power of praise. His admonition to the followers of Christ includes, “. . . be filled with the Spirit, speaking to one another in psalms and hymns and spiritual songs, singing and making melody in your heart to the Lord, (Ephesians 5:18[b]-19.) Urging us to praise God for everything, at all times was one of the Apostle’s strongest messages.

Because we do not give enough credence to the integrity of scripture, we suffer much more than we otherwise would. Our enemies of depression, obsessions, fearful bondages and abuses of many kinds shackle us when we could walk free by obeying the commandments and precepts Holy Writ extends.

For sure, God has layered life with many good gifts, along with abundant truth throughout Holy Writ. A reader of scripture knows clearly what is just and what is not just. The gift of living a just life is that the oil of gladness flows, blessing one’s self and others.

Science is bearing out the wisdom of God, which should not be surprising. My friend Eugene Wiesner, clinical psychologist and former professor at Montana State University, taught that compliance with the scriptural mandates to praise and rejoice brings a chemical change in the body which not only promotes cellular healing, but alleviates both physical pain and mental distress. During his practice, Dr. Wiesner said 40 percent of the people he treated were suffering with psychological disorders. Others needed therapy for fears, grief and guilt. He addressed the latter problems with what he called "God's psychology," telling patients to "sing the Psalms and rejoice in everyday living—through the hard times as well as the easy." Dr. Wiesner's premise was simple, "When people believe what God's Word says, and obey it, they get well!"

My own experience with depression took place when earlier in life my friend was murdered by her 14-year-old son. I made accusations toward God, feeling He had failed us. Unable to handle the intensity of my feelings, I opted for denial and slipped into intense depression and anxiety for several months. Medication helped. But, what truly brought a lasting healing was doing everything Dr. Wiesner told me to do through a few phone calls, which this generous, caring man allowed.

Much was learned as I developed the practice of praising and rejoicing, trusting in the reign of God regardless of circumstances. Soon, the walls of my prison came down. Walls of doubt, fear, shock and other elements of inner angst collapsed. Once restored, I began to believe with all my soul that God can and will turn all things to good. Humbled, I gradually grew in my belief that God is still in charge of the world, regardless of cruel tragedies that seem far too prevalent.

It felt like I had lost all my baby teeth at once. But never again will I resist abiding daily with a heart full of praise, for therein lies power and Presence, healing and hope. Practicing a praise-filled faith carries us like a thermal on which our souls do soar. Herein lies joy!

Who needs God?

Recently, we needed help for a household repair. A plan was in place for a carpenter to do the work. When Monday came, no carpenter at 7 a.m., but rather a phone call. The man apologized saying, "I am sick." I said, "We will pray for you." After a healthy pause, he asked, "What do you mean?"

It jarred me into realizing that offering prayer to a person who is sick and unaccustomed to prayer could take a person by surprise. Yet, let's get real. Our nation has superabundance. Most, is seems, live in a state of complacency, having all we need—and more than we need.

Prior to the COVID-19 virus's nasty appearance it is fair to say a majority in the nation did not have to suffer out of "needing" much of anything"—and didn't need God. Working hard and playing as often as possible kept schedules tight. And, those of us who are counting on God's help daily, also enjoyed the "benn-ies" of living "in the promise land" meaning the most powerful nation in the world. Now, may I also dare to say most likely a lot of people may be surprising themselves as they pray for God to help them through this pandemic? At least this can be our hope.

Perhaps many are now wondering, praying for this crisis to end . . . and may even be wanting to explore what it takes to live a righteous life. ("Righteous" means "right living" with the help of God.)

Those of us who study Scripture believe it is fool hardy to live life as if there is no God. Doing business with an attitude that our spiritual needs are "non-essential," virtually means, "who needs it?'

Truth be known none of us have much certainty as to what the future holds. What we can know for sure is that God wants to be in our lives and to help us through. Psalm 34:17-18, holds promise, "The righteous cry out, and the LORD hears, and delivers them out of all their troubles. The

Lord *is* near to those who have a broken heart, and saves such as have a contrite spirit."

The following poem by Margaret Halaska, a Roman Catholic Sister, is titled, "Covenant."

"The Father knocks at my door, seeking a home for his son:
Rent is cheap, I say
I don't want to rent. I want to buy, says God.
I'm not sure I want to sell,
but you might come in to look around.
I think I will, says God.
I might let you have a room or two.
I like it, says God. I'll take the two.
You might decide to give me more someday.
I can wait, says God.
I'd like to give you more,
but it's a bit difficult. I need some space for me.
I know, says God, but I'll wait. I like what I see.
Hmm, maybe I can let you have another room.
I really don't need that much.
Thanks, says God, I'll take it. I like what I see.
I'd like to give you the whole house
but I'm not sure –
Think on it, says God. I wouldn't put you out.
Your house would be mine and my son would live in it.
You'd have more space than you'd ever had before.
I don't understand at all.
I know, says God, but I can't tell you about that.
You'll have to discover it for yourself.
That can only happen if you let him have the whole house.
A bit risky, I say.
Yes, says God, but try me.

I'm not sure—
I'll let you know.

I can wait, says God. I like what I see."

Is it only for the birds?

The other day while at Rotary Park, my attention was drawn to a flock of birds. What must have been a hundred pair of beating wings flew toward me, then in a flick of a moment swept upward, did a switchback after a mid-air loop, dropping in for a gentle landing about 50 yards from my feet. As I watched this superb movement of the birds, it was a song of unity heard by my soul.

How did the birds know the "when" and the "where" of their unison flight? Not one missed a beat as they displayed total oneness. It was as if each followed the dictates of an omniscient, omnipresent mind. Harmony at its glorious best.

Moments before I had prayed, "Father, teach me your ways," and upon pondering the birds as they sat softly in the grass I thought of Jesus' prayer to the Father for His followers, "that they all may be one, as You, Father, *are* in Me, and I in You; that they also may be one in Us, that the world may believe that You sent Me," (John 17:21).

Until one reads the Gospel of John, Chapter 17, there is no way to understand the intentions of Jesus Christ . . . or, to comprehend the Kingdom of God He was extending to us as humans.

The Lord has a vision of unity for all who love Him— multitudes acting as one in perpetuating the Kingdom of God on earth. Imagine for a moment, a people so tuned-in to the needs of one another that a constant rushing in, pulling back, and flowing together would be seen, filling each and every gap as it appeared. A people able to lay aside the "whims" of personal wills. A people ever seeking the mind of Christ, preferring *His* will over their own. A global orchestra performing a masterpiece symphony, instilling peace, love and joy right here on Planet Earth.

What gets in our way of participating? Self-will? Ambition for making a name for one's self? Storing wealth beyond what can be used well? Or, stubbornness, thinking, "It's all about me." These are some of which create jealousy, competition and lack of care for what is best for all.

We all have attributes and ambitions. Yet, prideful behavior is a ubiquitous human tendency, arising out of wanting to control, or to be the one with the best plan, the one to do the directing, the giving of orders. Power-plays begin with elevating self and often result in back-biting. These create the opposite of unity: division, confusion, anger, even bitterness—anything but selfless love. This is a far cry from God's call for us to shine forth, being the "light the world," (See Matthew 5:14-16.)

For sure, we are going to have difficult human behaviors to deal with until the day we die, as none of us can get "all the dents out" before that moment of "departure" which we call "death." So, working on ourselves for the betterment is a lifetime project. The human conscience in itself is a wonderful thing when we are humble enough to be tuned into it, allowing for opportunities to frequently correct ourselves.

The call of Christ to His people has always been to grow in our being sensitive to the needs of others, not just among those who are our friends and family, but reaching out to touch the marginal people, or those in the tightest of life's places. For instance our nursing homes (or our shut-in neighbors) where there is little to do and people are lonely. A lot of contacts can be made by phone or email, in such a time as we are in.

Today, I wasn't "in the flow." I occasionally play policeman of the world, if only in my thoughts. While in the park I had great and wondrous thoughts—even said some prayers. Then, along came a woman with a dog having no leash on her pet. I couldn't keep my mouth shut. Then, not long after that, I was standing ready to pay for a purchase when a woman with a child moved right up beside me. I was irked because we have a 6' rule during this global crises. Well, guess what. I wasn't patient about it. Back at the car, I regretted my stance in the situation and prayed, "Lord, I'll bet there is something you would like to say to me, right now."

Some days I do better at "picking up the cross" and carrying it, again and again. Our asking forgiveness and granting forgiveness to ourselves and to others will bring us closer to laying down our judgements and mistrusts—of God, yes, but also of ourselves and others.

For sure, following Christ does call for a certain "death to self" in order for God's people to form a safe and joyous flight creating a universal oneness that sees each as being instrumental in life's symphonic concert. Perhaps, adding, on occasion, a good ol' hootenanny.

Signs of this are even now "in the air." There is a lot of good care going on for one another, bringing hope for a future of living together with a new kind of closeness—perhaps a felt unity through experiencing our current, shared suffering within a society that surely needs fresh hope for unity and peace.

Wisdom . . . a gift from God

A young woman recently said, "I love God, but He doesn't always love me."

Had it been a more appropriate time I would have said something about the error of projecting our own feelings onto God. Doing so robs us of peace which is rightfully ours—and more.

Knowing this young woman, I am aware of her battle to conquer habits and desires that are causing her dismay. How different might her struggle be if she could feel assured of God's abiding love?

Most of us are more kind to others in comparison to the way we treat ourselves. Many times we fail to love ourselves and sometimes we become our own worst enemy. Human tendency can be to whine and blame, projecting all kinds of negative stuff toward God. Therefore, we think God surely cannot love us either. After all, look at our mistakes! In finding it difficult to accept ourselves and to forgive ourselves for our faults, we judge God according to our own limitations.

It is vital to know where we stand, being certain of God as a loving Father. A Father whose love does not stop. Period. When others have departed and we suffer self-doubt, God sticks with us maintaining compassion. No wonder at times we neglect to read Holy Writ. Our esteem of self can be so low we can't risk hoping to hear from God. What is happening is that He loves us and wants us to have His wisdom. God's wisdom and God's love are synergistic and inseparable.

Granted, we deserve chastisement at times. Our actions can become like a testy child who cries out. A reprimand can be God's best gift to us. But instead of withholding His love, in the very act of chastising, God claims us as His own. It takes wisdom to see when chastisement is coming down the pike. When we are living a prayerful life, we know pretty much instantly. "Oops! I should not have done that!"

It is not wise to trust in ourselves or our own strength. Many failures come as a result. Does it sound too lofty a goal, to seek and find the wisdom of God?

There are many passages of Scripture which indicate God's wisdom is there for the asking. While doing a topical study on "wisdom," I found a distinction between the various types. Natural wisdom includes identifying and applying natural abilities like technical and mechanical. Natural wisdom also includes the arts—and the healing arts. Worldly wisdom involves philosophies based on certitudes of the world. Then, there is the wisdom that comes from God.

There is a strong New Testament warning for those who think they are wise: "Who *is* wise and understanding among you? Let him show by good conduct *that* his works *are done* in the meekness of wisdom . . . [For] the wisdom that is from above is first pure, then peaceable, gentle, willing to yield, full of mercy and good fruits, without partiality and without hypocrisy," (James 3: 13 and17).

Sadly, most of us live short of our potential either because we do not know God's will or do not believe His promises are what we can lay claim to and live into. Therefore, we begin to believe we can trust what "we think" is true. (This is getting close to "magical thinking.") In other words, we can devise "our own truth." This is not wise and moves us into deception; we can end up going down trails that are off the beaten paths of truth. Getting real busy with what *appears* important—at times when we are not considering Scripture as our guide, it is easy to make choices based on what seems OK, as it fits well with what we want . . . or, "feels" right.

Yet, this only finds us sifting through hay, wood and stubble neglecting the very great good that God has for us. That is the truth we find when we spend time reading Scripture, which believers receive as "God's Word" to us—intended to enlighten and elucidate our way. This is how we grow closer to God.

Natural wisdom that we see portrayed in nature is amazing—yet, not intended to be worshiped. After all, you can't worship something that's not greater than yourself. Nature is here to provide for us and for us to enjoy.

Worldly wisdom, as mentioned above is all about our choosing what "feels right," or it is based on the desire to be liked, praised, appreciated—*seen* as above the ordinary. These are pride based and can lead to a lot of foolishness, in opposition to what comes to us when we devote our lives to "hearing from God." In that regard, the Scriptures absolutely fascinate those who really get "into it."

If we Christians truly seek to know truth, we find it between the pages of Genesis through Revelations. We know it as "the truth of God." And, when we live "by the book" we are on solid ground, avoiding sinking sands. We find the guidance of rules that reflect the righteousness of God, rules that have holding power, keeping us in safe stead—out of trouble. With that, we find the peace that only our Lord can give. And, we gain an ability to love with God's objective love, rather than a subjective love based on what feels right in the moment, or what others in the world think, believe and would prefer that we follow.

Generation after generation have settled for various poor substitutes for what is God's best. That is, except for those who live by "the Book." They are not too hard to spot. "You will know them by their fruits," (Matthew 7:16).

Utilizing neglected power

The power to focus is something with which the aging process surely does a dance. In the past, while listening to a televised sermon, a strange thing happened. An overlay of sound came across nearly drowning out the pastor's voice. By some technical blooper, two events were coming across at once.

It was not easy going, but as long as I concentrated, purposely blocking out the intruding somewhat louder sound, I could clearly understand the more desirable message. After several minutes of this I became rather surprised and pleased that by tightly focusing I could block out one message in order to hear the other.

How similar this is to the "spiritual hearing" within our daily experience of following Christ. The sounds of the world come through loud and clear: alarms, distress, expectations, demands, and the many, ever-present yearnings of our varied appetites. Yet, when we are prayerfully listening, the message of God is alive and strong, heard deep within our hearts. This involves continually choosing what we want to hear. It takes keen development of our power to focus while overriding the "never-resting" voices of our times.

It seems there are five voices we hear predominantly: 1) our own with our delights, disdains and desires, 2) the world's, as already mentioned, 3) Satan, the deceiver's voice with his temptations and accusations, 4) the voices of those closest to us, 5) the voice of God. Christians who seek maturity learn to recognize which is which. We can become keenly adept, as well, in examining the motives that lie beneath our choices and actions.

This is no easy task, but possible as we depend on the empowerment and grace of God along with the guidance of the Holy Spirit. With our minds focusing on Him and our ears in tune with His voice we can live in the world with peace, no matter what goes on around us, even though the world lives literally in our laps, given modern media with all its perplexities!

Staying tuned into God can best see us hearing His voice, doing His will. Sometimes that will find us sharing of our means. Other times, we will be humble while allowing others to help us. Most of us are exceedingly blessed. Any feelings of guilt for having been blessed can be dismissed, as surely God is greatly pleased when his children prosper. For the more we prosper, the more we are able to give—not only of our substance, but from the "fruit of our lips," meaning the praise and thanksgiving offered up as we rejoice in the goodness of the Lord.

There are at least 150 references to "rejoicing" according to Cruden's Concordance. Scriptural references to "praise" are even more numerous, not to mention all that is recorded about offering "thanksgiving." We are even told to praise when things seem to be going wrong! With this in mind, let's ask ourselves how much of our mental energies are given to such efforts?

Dr. Eugene Wiesner, a Catholic psychologist from Billings, Montana, claims the key to good mental health depends on rejoicing, being thankful and full of praise. He makes an outstanding statement. While holding up his Bible, the good doctor plants a thumb on top and says, “There is more psychology under my thumb than in all the books that line the shelves of my library." Within his teachings, this psychologist claims rejoicing in the Lord can supersede depression, especially when praises to God are sung. There is power in song!

Every tool needed for coping is generously supplied in Scripture. We have only to search them out and put them into practice.

All of us, at times, are guilty of bonding a bit with the world . . . even to entertain evil thoughts. (Hurtful treatment of others is undoubtedly one of the worst of all evils.) When we are judgmental far too often we speak hurtful words. Once there, a believer knows she or he has fallen short. Next comes shame for having slipped up—and not being able to “take it back.” Guilt or self-condemnation follow.

In order to maintain a healthy mental climate, we best allow the wind of the Holy Spirit to sweep our minds continually. "Godward" glances in moments of stress or temptation, coupled with pleas for the Spirit's guidance, sees us in prayerful submission seeking the cleansing power of Christ. Now, back in right standing, we are in tight fellowship, again, with Father God. How wonderful it is to be forgiven!

We are not going to be able to control what the days, weeks and months bring as life rolls on, but we can control our thoughts. 2 Corinthians 10:4-5, admonishes “. . . the weapons of our warfare *are* not carnal but mighty in God for pulling down strongholds, casting down arguments and every high thing that exalts itself against the knowledge of God, bringing every thought into captivity to the obedience of Christ . . . .”

For me, one of the greatest challenges in life is to become more discerning and more God-empowered within my thought processes. For as the saying goes, “We aren't what we think we are, but we are what we think.”

Afraid of dying?

As explained earlier, I had a hard time staying alive between the ages of 13-35. First, I had encephalitis with very high temperatures for days with sleeping sickness. Then at age 18, I started forming blood clots in my legs and abdomen. There were many episodes of these clots breaking loose and travelling into my heart, landing in my lungs. Eventually, my condition worsened and the doctor said, "Your lungs cannot survive another assault."

The surgeon and cardiologist stood at my bedside explaining my chances of living beyond this point were virtually nil. They described a new surgical procedure. Yet, since this type of surgery was unique and innovative to the medical field, little hope was offered for a good outcome. Gary and I prayed for guidance; we decide to take the chance of the surgery saving my life.

My Christian faith was strong. I knew if I died heaven would be my next destination. Strangely, what I feared was being placed in a grave. Through my years of dealing with pulmonary emboli (clots in lungs) I had prayed, "God, please don't let me die during the winter." I knew the climate where we lived would mean being buried in a cold grave, topped with snow.

During the three days of waiting for the surgery, I had a vision. I saw a dark, heavy-tempered gate with the word "DEATH" at its top. I was afraid, trembling in my bed. But, then I could suddenly see the opposite side of that gate. It was a great and glorious pearl from heaven's side. A "little girl" danced up to the opening and said, "Just step across!" She had a great smile and beckoned me, saying, "It is just one step." Although she coached me several times, I could not take that step. But, this vision ended my fear of the grave. I realized I am not my body and I will have only to step through the gate when death comes.

I did survive the life-saving surgery and recovered. One day while driving my car, I suddenly saw a part of that vision, once again, and knew in an instance something about the little girl. It was as if I was being divinely told, "That is your daughter"—and I knew, without a doubt, this is true. Years earlier, I had a miscarriage between my first and second sons. Nearly three decades had passed when my heart prompted me to receive the truth: The vision had allowed the little girl I wanted, yet could not hold in my womb, to minister to me that night when I was so close to death.

From then on, I knew even more surely there is a heaven and this precious little girl is waiting for when I will "cross over."

The beautiful part is that I was given many more years, as the surgery was highly successful. I lived to raise my family and to enjoy a long, loving relationship with my dear husband, Gary.

I am now getting close to the time when people normally die. I know death is coming, yet I have no fear at all. It's like knowing a trip is around the corner. However, on this trip I cannot take anything with me, not even the costly crowns on my teeth. So, I pray to do all possible to become all that God knew I could be when He first saw me conceived. I also believe none of us get to be entirely finished—totally ready to meet our Maker. We have flawed natures, which most likely we will be trying to conquer when we draw our last breath.

The wonderful news is that the Lord Jesus has forgiven our sins. Upon repentance of them, we are washed to the core, cleansed— ready for eternity.

"For God hath not appointed us to wrath, but to obtain salvation by our Lord Jesus Christ, who died for us, that whether we wake or sleep, we should live together with Him. Wherefore comfort each other and edify one another just, as you also are doing," *(*1 Thessalonians 5:9-11*).*

Have you heard the "midnight cry?"

It was dark. We lost our power. My friend touched a match to the fuel of her lantern and immediately we had light with which to face the coming darkness. How grateful I was to be invited to her cabin, knowing she would be prepared for all eventualities.

I am reminded of Jesus' parable of the five foolish virgins and the five wise virgins of Matthew 25:1-13. All had lamps and all had fallen asleep. But the difference between the wise and the foolish lies in the fact that it is not enough to have a lamp. This parable shows the need for our lamps to carry oil. The crux of the matter seems to be about having a fresh supply of oil. What else could this mean other than Jesus pointing out His hope for us to be filled up with the indwelling presence of the Holy Spirit?

It is interesting to note that the five foolish virgins *did* have oil to start with, but they had let it run dry. That is like us today if we trust in a profession of faith made in the past, but have fallen asleep on it, letting our light grow dim, then out.

Each one of us has fallen asleep at some point in time. But the wise of this parable woke up, trimmed their lamps, filled them with oil, and as Jesus put it "… those who were ready and went with Him to the wedding; and the door was shut," (Matthew 25:10).

I wonder if what we are living and experiencing today indicates we are getting close to history's darkest hour—midnight. A time when perpetual wrong decisions could bring destruction to all humanity. This is a time when terrorism and crime abound and men find their hearts failing them for fear. Perhaps, as many are predicting, including scientists, we are facing the final act on history's stage. If so, it is not a time to panic or hide from reality, but to rejoice, knowing full well God is in control. He has a plan for His people!

It is a time to "clean our chimneys" (confessing our sins), trim our wicks (repenting of our bad attitudes, resentments, pettiness and general lack of love) and ask God to fill us with His Holy Spirit. This is not something someone else can give us, as is clearly seen in the parable when the five foolish virgins begged the wise ones for oil. Being filled with the Holy Spirit is the Lord's gift to us. Then Jesus said, "I am the light of the world. He who follows Me shall not walk in darkness, but have the light of life," (John 8:12).

How to get lit? All we have to do is ask. The parable plainly shows there will be a time when it is too late to ask for the oil of the Holy Spirit.

I recently heard the story of three apprentice devils. They put their heads together with Satan discussing how they might deceive the people of the earth. One suggested they perpetrate the lie, "There is no God." Satan said, "No. That is stupid. Almost everyone suspects there is a God."

The second little devil said, "I know, we will tell them God is dead." Satan said, "No. That will never work." The third little devil fairly bounced with glee said, "I've got it! We'll tell them there's no hurry!"

May God help us to hear our "midnight cry" and be swift to awaken and make ready for what Scripture indicates will be the coming of the Bridegroom (Christ) to receive His Bride (those who have committed their lives to Christ).

Attending to the "signs of the time" will prompt us to have "oil in their lamps and not be afraid of what is "seen" in the news or worried about the concerns of the world. Scripture may seem metaphorical with readers not knowing what to grasp as the intended meaning. But for believers, God will give us all we need to know as we walk in faith. On the other hand, being knowledgeable and voting makes us good citizens

Believers who follow Christ's teachings do carry His Spirit within—wherever we go. Being watchful, seeing the "signs," knowing that this "gospel of the kingdom will be preached in all the world as a witness to all nations, and then the end will come," (Matthew 24:14).

So, Christ will return to the earth as Scriptures make clear. What a glorious event it will be when the many hundreds of biblical references, scholars have seen as predicators, are suddenly fulfilled. For sure, Jesus' Second Coming will be the most magnanimous and numinous occasion of history—beyond anything anyone can imagine.

Contemplating the ageless sands

While sitting at the ocean's edge many thoughts ran through my head. But mostly the question—*what is the mystical message being said by the sea?*

Covering over one third the planet's surface, the Pacific Ocean rocks and rolls in its bed. The Creator set up the seas, so beautiful—and in perpetual motion. Awesome, reverent, nourishing, steadfast and persistent. These are all adjectives one might use in describing God.

The seas. Signs of His love. Without these planned entities of provision, we could not live. Glorious sights to see . . . symbols of the arms of God, wherein one does not run without due respect and preparation.

Wonder-filled moments were spent watching the surge and draw of ocean's song. A message that would sweep to greater depths in this person's soul . . . as time was given to listening. Sitting for days, toes nudging deep in warm, wet sand, gradually words surfaced to interpret emotions stirred by the sea.

As usual, questions come. Why is the ocean salty? Turning to the "knowledge of the ages"—good old encyclopedia: "Rocks of the earth's crust, disintegrated by weathering, released their salt to streams, to rivers and eventually enter the seas." Sands, saturated with the sacred, both wonderful and electrifying at the same time.

I sit with feet planted in trillions of specks of mineral and rock which have been whisked slowly from all parts of the world. I think of my own minuteness.

Here today, "as the grass of the fields," scripture describes mankind. But tomorrow, wilted and gone with the sun's heat. There on the seashore the meaning of these words reach the center of my soul. I am but a tiny speck in an incomprehensible universe, which is itself a tiny speck in a vast sea of galaxies. Hardly noticeable when viewed in the scope of it all. Yet of such value Jesus Christ, God's own Son, came to this earth to die for the likes of me, and you—redeeming us back to where we belong . . . in intimate fellowship with the Father.

It seems incredible to personalize that monumental act of sacrifice and love on the part of Almighty God. Still, from the beginning, "the plan" was always about making a way for us to live an intimate, cherished relationship with Him.

Yet, the only way it can have meaning is if it is brought home to personal souls. Then having entered into the dance of acceptance, we say, "Yes" to who God has called us to be. We embrace the unspeakable privilege of receiving "the right to become children of God," (John 1:12).

It is through Him that we are truly "something." Yes, by laying down our need to "be something" we are empowered with the truth of who we truly are intended to be. Such awareness brings freedom. Freedom to truly step onto the turf of being shaped and formed by the Holy Spirit of God. It takes humility to rely on and rest in that.

Growing into our potentials as sons and daughters of the Most High God happens because of our decision to invite Him in. In this, we become indwelled by Him, tiny replicas of His love on earth. What once were mere specks of human substance become living stones "built up in a spiritual house, a holy priesthood." Here, in the now, we become" spiritual sacrifices acceptable to God by Jesus Christ," (1 Peter 2:5).

Pregnant with hope and faith we become agents of love . . . vessels of clay filled with holy treasure. No longer caught up in self-seeking ventures hoping for peace—grasping for happiness. Rather, to be merged with His redemptive act of sacrifice, united with all saints throughout the earth. For all believers from times passed to time present are as the sands of the sea, myriad in number and saturated with the sacred.

A salty, holy people of God, who "partake of the abundance of the seas and of treasures hidden in the sands," (Deuteronomy 33:19).

What's to be gained?

Yesterday, I eyed Gary's sharp-looking, "gym" jeans thinking maybe they would fit me. He watched as I was stepping into them, defying gravity with strategic maneuvers. Of course, I heard his words, "They aren't going to fit!"

Well, guess what, they didn't. I was chagrined while trying to pull the zipper up. "Butt" . . . due to the winds of time that was not going to happen. The sands have shifted on this body of mine.

The truth is this: Not being able to work out at the gym for weeks on end—plus being in a bit of shock over what's happening worldwide—has no doubt brought these shifted sands to many a "bod" faster than we could imagine. That was a mouthful, but I have to start laughing about it so as to ward off disparagement. At least the bathroom mirror hasn't cracked, yet, as I peer into it.

Yes, Gary and I are still able to talk sweetly to one another and enjoy our days together. Not yet tempted to go "screaming into the desert, such as people joke about doing." After all, we are told by the Governor, *stay home and hang in there!* What helps by yards and miles is to keep our focus. We know this won't last forever, it just seems like it will. The best way to get through this, no matter what else goes on in history, is to focus on what is true. Philippians 4:8, for instance instructs us to monitor our thoughts based on, ". . . whatever things are true, whatever things are noble, whatever things are just, whatever things are pure, whatever things are lovely, whatever things are of good report, if there is any virtue and if there is anything praiseworthy—meditate on these things."

The greatest of all truths is found in Scripture.

What on earth might be lovelier than the baby quails just now seen running and hiding amongst the shrubs, right here at home?

Rabbits are everywhere, some jumping over each other. Watching them supports saneness during this most unusual time of living with uncertainties that we dare not let our minds play with. Yet, God has given us a wonderful world and much within it is "of good report." Noble people abide, here, with us. Like those at the Havasu Community Food Bank who risk their own safety as they hand out food to hungry people.

It seems doubtful there is anyone alive on the globe that has seen days wherein outings to the grocery store become the highlight of a day, a great quest to discover *what's available today*. It seems the pandemic has lasted for months forcing changes, blocking our usual pattern of living. Yet, thank God for Lake Havasu City's gorgeous lake, mountains and sunny days. Walks in the park find us wondering why we haven't done this more often throughout our 29 years of living here! Now, there is time . . . time to ponder what is most important in life. It is also a time during which most of us can get more rest—and consequently, take on more pounds.

While trying to stay fit for our jeans, the most fitting of all things is to abide in Christ by savoring the beauty of His Word. Think of the profoundness that comes through a verse like Romans 8:28, that truly fits our situation, "And we know that all things work together for good to those who love God, to those who are the called according to *His* purpose."

A passage read this morning brought the Psalmist, David, back to mind. He said to the Lord, "My times are in your hand." We, too, are going through a battle of sorts while knowing life could be at stake. Yet, a much different one from King David and the battles he faced alongside his armies. We can't *see* our enemy. It may be the *fear of what we cannot see* that brings the unnerving question, "what is happening to us right now?" Every time we open a computer or laptop pictures of the coronavirus are there. The other day, I caught myself washing my hands after closing the lid. Thoughts of hoping to escape the COVID-19 virus are ubiquitous—and we certainly don't want this virus to rise its thorny little head as we blissfully sleep come nighttime.

This is new to us! I remember my Dad saying as encouragement when I was afraid to try something new. He would watch and say, "That's the stuff!" as I progressed. Truth be known God is watching over us. In 2 Timothy 1:7, Scripture says, "God has not given the spirit of fear, but of power and of love and of a sound mind." That's the truth we best keep in mind.

So God has "the stuff" and surely we need not lament the fact that lack of action now finds us stuffing ourselves into our "comfies." The best thought to hold is *we are not hungry* . . . at least probably not in Lake Havasu City. We have our notable Food Bank—proof that the most generous people on earth live here!

Last week, a "little bird" told me something truly awesome. She works at the Food Bank and here are her words, "Incredible news! Today at the Food Bank we had more donations than clients! There was a line of people with cars full of donated food and checks. People were signing over their stimulus checks to us saying they did not need them, knowing we do." Faith in humanity is restored. God is good and the people in this town are very generous!

Now, this fits for keeping our mind on good stuff!

The making of precious gems

Life is full of irritations, large and small. People and circumstances can aggravate, and sometimes frustrate us. We would not be human otherwise. Yet our responses have lasting effects.

This is best seen in the lowly oyster. When a foreign body like a grain of sand, an undeveloped egg or a parasite finds its way into the oyster's shell a secretion is stimulated. Layer upon layer of this material called "mother of pearl," coats the invader eventually creating a beautiful gem.

Since ancient times, pearls have been considered to be among the most precious gems. This is probably the reason the word "pearl" is used metaphorically for anything of great value, particularly in the scriptures. Truth be told, we have continual opportunities to make "pearls" by coating our "irritants" through seeking to be patient with people and situations. Recovery, even from the hardest of circumstances, comes through forgiveness and prayer.

When a personal relationship goes awry the temptation is to reject the person, isolating our self from him or her. Yet, Jesus teaches a better way, instructing us to communicate, reaching change when this can be done . . . while forgiving what hurts and accepting what cannot be changed.

Have you noticed how making a decision to forgive is not a onetime occurrence? The memory of the smarting offense returns again and again. But, by continually reminding ourselves that we have forgiven and by praying often for ourselves and the offenders, we make gems out of what otherwise would remain as sharp irritants, ever present to annoy. The choice is ours.

We do not have the power to do this in our own strength. It takes grace—a grace that God can give making it possible to forgive and to continue to love. The way we gain that grace comes most easily through finding time to be with God in prayer.

Jesus routinely left the crowds and sought isolated spots where He could enjoy conversing with His Father. The results are recorded for all to read … a trail of gems. He was empowered to embrace the rebuffs and other hardships within His earthly ministry. How? By continually reaching out in forgiveness and love – all the way to the cross.

Next week Lent begins. For those who observe Lent, the six weeks prior to Easter Sunday are spent reflecting more deeply on who Jesus is and what He accomplished on our behalves. It becomes a sacred part of the year, with time set aside to be alone with God. It is a time during which ideally, our dedication to Christ is deepened. This may mean getting up a half hour or an hour earlier than usual, or taking time in the evening in a place where quietude can be found.

Jesus asked this of His disciples, "Come aside by yourselves to a deserted place and rest a while," (Mark 6:31a).

In the quiet moments while reading God's Word and listening to Him speak deep within, we find strength, purpose and guidance. We find grace—"mother of pearl"— for the making of gems. Pearls . . . appropriate gifts for Christ, the King of all who seek to live His teachings.

Is "belonging" something to seek?

Two appaloosa colts ran about ever so carefree in my father's pasture. They were beautiful and Dad seemed to have done a good job with them. I recall, here, what my father said back then, while still alive and working in his corral:

"You know those colts of mine? While watching them the other day, I realized the relationship between my belonging to God and those horses belonging to me.

"I am responsible for those horses. I bought them, paid for them. Put them in my pasture. I irrigate that pasture, bring in hay, mend the fences, and meet all their needs. And, I know if I am going to use those horses, I will have to train them. "

Dad said, "This is the way it is with God. He has bought us with the blood of His Son, Jesus Christ. Now, if we truly trust in His redemption—act as if we belong to Him, obey His commands—He will take care of our every need. He will even be able to prepare us for His use."

The conversation with Dad was relevant to the circumstances in Gary's and my life at that time. Gary had just lost his job. After working as a ticket agent for Greyhound since age 18 for 26 years. He lost his job, along with all Greyhound station employees; the Boise terminal became a commissioned agency.

Gary was designated as the commissioned agent to operate the terminal going forward. I helped with a few light duties; so the two of us worked arduously during the following seven weeks. However, after 26 years with Greyhound, Gary decided 12-16 hour days seven days a week was too much.

We could not envision living our lives that way, so we paid our bills, said our "goodbyes" and closed the book on Greyhound. At age 44, Gary began doing the college scene "with a six-pack of Geritol." For the next four years he was a fulltime student at Boise State University studying in the field of radiology.

Having a paycheck all those years was a bit addicting. And, while grappling with readjusting, I remembered Dad's words, "If we really belong to God—I mean *really* belong to Him, and are giving Him what He paid for—we are *His* responsibility and not our own."

Psalm 91 speaks of dwelling in a place of trust, "abiding in the shelter of the Almighty," a place of total dependence on a Master who provides and protects. These are words we have read often, yet can be more readily embraced and understood once our will becomes aligned with the will of our Master. It is like when the gate is down . . . work done . . . and whistling is heard. New pastures become known.

We are creatures of comfort and unless God allows some pressure to be applied we do not grow. Unlike the ponies in Dad's pasture, we are made in the likeness and image of God, called and chosen, charted for a course to become the mature children of God spoken of in John 1:12.

About the time we settle in, thinking we have gained some ground, our faith is tested and often found wanting.

The Apostle Paul described believers as being changed, "From glory to glory," through the trials of life. We become more patient, more humble and malleable. As we turn our angst and uncertainty over to Him, our Heavenly Father turns it all to gain. We are trusted; chosen for training and equipping—soon to serve others.

He is looking for our total trust. Otherwise, why would this be the most repeated command of Scripture, "Do not be afraid," and the most frequent promise, "I will be with you"?

Father, help me to *really* trust You. Teach me Your ways. Grant me the grace to follow Your will rather than to jump fences, kick up my heels and go my own willful way.

Faith, like muscle, requires exercise

After 911, Stacey Randall wrote, "A Loving Tribute," a poem in which Jesus is saying, "I will be in the stairwell of your final moments." We all remember the stories of how among the few who survived that terrifying time in the stairwell of the North Tower had a sense of the Lord being right there with them. They knew they were not alone.

Last August, our youngest son had open heart surgery. In view of other serious health problems, I tried to prepare myself, should he not survive. I feared my own heart would cave in if the news any parent fears should need to be heard.

"He has so much more life to live; please God intervene," was my prayer. As Gary and I waited long hours, it was as if I could barely breathe or think. Then from deep within, I heard, "I am here with you." Strength, comfort and fresh hope arose. Rejoicing came with the doctor's report, "Two bypasses—and His heart is pumping on its own." We were assured the next few days would be "ify." But, happily, our son is with us today!

Many of us have known times of feeling like we are about to "cave in," yet were given an inner sense of not being here on the globe alone. Rather, we felt joined by the Almighty One, who is fully able to make "the necessary happen." And, God alone knows what that is.

Are you noticing how each time we go through a trial, we come out stronger? Oswald Chambers put it this way, "The trial of our faith gives us a good banking account in the heavenly places, and when the next trial comes our wealth there will tide us over. If we have confidence in God beyond the actual . . . we shall see the lie at the heart of the fear, and our faith will win through in every detail."

That heavenly bank account does at times seem way too small. Still, there is always enough for what is needed—if we hold steady and pray our way through. Jesus has told us to "pray always." This way, we can stop short of panicking.

All of the above is about growing spiritual muscle, which is something we do not get by curling up in the corner fretting in fear of losses. It comes in exercising our faith, thrusting it over and over into the face of our fears.

Doing battle with fear is not easy as fear is an awesome boxer. Especially when our tendencies lean toward, "seeing is believing." So, when we "do not" see signs of getting what we hope for, and when the odds seem entirely against us, it is easy to start losing our footing.

This battle is common to us all, but especially so when our children are involved. Countless times, while raising three sons, I have taken a troubling matter to God, while visualizing the act of putting the situation "on the altar." (Remember Abraham's great moment of putting his son there?) Then, I renege. My mind never seems to stop its efforts to "figure it all out." I slip into varied mental gyrations. Waiting patiently gets passed by with my intense desire to "do something to fix it" more quickly. Waiting on God might take too long, right?

Spiritual battles call for growth. Persistence is gained as we work our way through them. There are times when it seems our backs are against the ropes and we find ourselves hanging on with all our might. With battered emotions, we remember to call on God. We may even recall a Scripture like, "Lo, I am with you always."[3] Strength comes! We stop gasping for breath and face up to that "ol' enemy" in the ring. Placing our trust afresh in the Lord strengthens our resolve and provides a "second wind."

It is through winning the battle over fear that we truly are able to live on a higher level of reality. While in those tight and fearsome places we learn to look beyond actualities, and stay focused on the powerful truths of Scripture that bolster our faith—like, "Be strong and of good courage; be not afraid or dismayed. The Lord your God is with you wherever you go," (Joshua 1:9).

[3] Matthew 28:20 New King James V

How to handle our anger and fear

Last week, while watching national news the coverage was upsetting. What was shown seemed unbelievable. Even ominous—as I pondered it. I felt helpless while watching our national capitol sieged and under attack on January 6, 2021. I sat praying while feeling numb and rocked back. Then anger and grief were felt, as well. It was hard handling all these difficult emotions on top of one another.

Throughout the day I turned to God in prayer, pleading for our country's well-being and safety. I prayed for peace and to forsake my arising fears. It was an emotional rollercoaster. Trying to think about anything else was difficult as disquieting thoughts surfaced persistently.

"We have to own up to our feelings," is a lesson learned through life and my work as a mental health counselor. Prayer became my best match for all the emotion felt. I was reminded to pray for myself first, then for all involved. Amazing the change that comes through caring and praying for others, while setting aside the tendency to be judgmental.

Anger is a challenging emotion. I, like many others, grew up believing anger was bad, something to avoid, or at least hide. Feelings were denied, pushed down deep inside. The reasons for this were in part due to messages perceived incorrectly, like "If you are a good Christian you won't get angry." Beyond that, to a child it can seem like "dangerous business" to show ire.

Unfortunately, in many homes there is little teaching on how to effectively deal with difficult emotions. The results? The gulping down of feelings, which is hazardous behavior both emotionally and physically. Ideally, we come to deal with the truth of Ephesians 4:26-27, where Paul instructs, "Be angry, and do not sin': do not let the sun go down on your wrath, nor give place to the devil."

We are expected to feel these feelings and to honor them by admitting the feelings to ourselves and to God. The verse continues with, "Do not let the sun go down on your wrath, nor give place to the devil." Here, we see God's desire for us to let Him help us move beyond our anger, our hurt feelings, the shock and awe of dangerous and difficult happenings—and to do so before we close our eyes to sleep. This makes sense from a psychological stance, as in this way we do not let it settle securely into our subconscious mind—where it is hard to heal.

But what about all those early years during which some of us denied anger, slept on it, and let it creep down into the cerebral grooves giving root to bitterness? Is there hope for its safe release so we can be free of its affecting our future?

According to one psychologist, Eugene Wiesner of Billings, Montana who for decades taught workshops on "God's Psychology," the answer is "yes." He explains that old, tamped-down anger must be allowed to surface and come to healing. How does that happen? By forgiving our enemies. And, forgiving everything that has hurt us in life. What good can come of hanging on to all that old stuff? It serves only to burn the soul like an acid.

So, rather than to avoid situations that trigger the anger or fall into old patterns of sullenness or resentment, he advises looking at that old pain each time it arises, then setting the will afresh to let it go. That is forgiveness. And, that is healing. Life is a learning experience—and God expects us to mature spiritually as we increase in years.

Then when the battle gets hot, and much is surfacing, calling for help through prayer carries tremendous power, and can put finishing touches on the task. One many multitudes of people have used throughout history is "The Jesus Prayer.[4]"

---

[4] If you want The "Jesus Prayer" go to my website at www.healinglifespain.com and click on "Quick Aids." A list drops down wherein this prayer can be found.

Wiesner taught that each time difficult feelings are triggered it is healing to simply ask Jesus to succor us as we lift these up to Him. In this way, given time, our souls become free from all the buried wrath and sorrows.

He told of dealing with frequently explosive feelings toward one of his sons. Yet, after working for three years with his emotions and using the "Jesus Prayer," Finally, he found the patience and endurance longed for. Wiesner said, "I eventually came to love my son unconditionally."

Through the years, I, too, learned that persevering in the hard work of inner healing, included choosing to persistently forgive the painful happenings of life. This sees me no longer at the mercy of my emotions. Jesus taught us to forgive, even to pray for our enemies. Doing so may seem like a hard pill to swallow, but it is good medicine, as it brings peace to one's heart.

A portrait of the Father—the One who created us

How do we come to know God who is Father and Creator of all? The One who's vocalized words we have yet to hear? This One who we have never seen? One whose hand we've never touched?

A little story told by a friend bears a poignant point.

A man, a self-proclaimed atheist stayed home by the fire on Christmas Eve while his wife attended mass. Idly, he wandered to the window and stared into the darkness, lit softly by moon and snow. A flock of birds pecked about for food around his porch.

Knowing it would be slim pickings he took some bird seed to the front door, sprinkled it about and waited. But, fear forced the birds to keep distance.

Back inside, the man went again to the window. He thought, "Maybe I could sprinkle seed in the garage and open the door. With the light on, they might see the seed, enter, eat and be warm." But the birds, fearful of such a huge being, could not trust his plan or follow his lead.

Then, caught by enthusiasm, the man thought: "If only I could become a bird! I could lead them easily. They would understand what I want of them; they would no longer be afraid."

Suddenly, he came face to face with the meaning of Christmas, saying: "This is what God achieved through Jesus." He realized by becoming human, the Father could have an intimate connection with those whom He loves—even to eat, laugh and dance with them. Most of all, He could teach them His ways and demonstrate His plan.

The simple story of a man who cared for birds displays the longing heart of the One who loves us. It was through sending Jesus that Father God could come to move, walk and talk revealing Himself and His great love.

He told us how to "come in out of the cold," and enter the kingdom of warmth by giving up our fears, our need to control, our tendencies to manipulate, so that we can accept the righteousness, peace and joy provided by His Spirit. He came to bring us freedom. And He introduced us to the Father by saying, "Anyone who has seen me has seen the Father."

A few months ago, I prayed earnestly to receive a clear concept of this Father who loved us that much. I wanted to comprehend – if only to the smallest degree—something about his personality.

I began an exercise which powerfully opened my eyes. It is one anyone can try. Make a list of the people who have most inspired or helped you in life. The "heroes," the teachers, closest friends who are vividly ensconced in your memory. Carefully identify the characteristics experienced with each one of these people.

Now, write the characteristics you saw in each one. This can form a portrait—a portrait of the Father, the one who created us. Each of the characteristics, each talent, gift and ability we admire or have benefited from within others was first a part of Him, imparted for the common good of all.

For me, two hours were spent, identifying all the characteristics and giftedness I have ever seen or heard of in any and all who came to mind while working steadily with pen and paper.

It is awesome, trying to envision One Being with all of these attributes while attempting to capture a glimpse of God, the Father of life and love. Imagine it: He is sincere, honest, stable, a master of excellence; He is creative, inventive, ingenuous and resourceful; He is fruitful, productive and diligent; He is enthusiastic, warm and caring; He is witty and musical—able to laugh and treasure intimate moments; He is supportive yet challenging—firm but fair; He is affirming, generous and winsome. These are surely only a few of God's attributes.

Attempting glimpses of God, can bring the possibility of a new appreciation for every person we encounter. Each one who walks this earth, holds a bit of God's Self waiting to be discovered. Finding these glimpses of God's essence in others can become a testament of His presence within each one of us. Of course, we are not God. Not perfect. Because of this, there are lots of opportunities to do the God-like thing: forgive and continue to love. In the very first page of the Bible, Genesis

1: 26-27, it stated explicitly that God has made us "in His own image." We have the great quest of living up to what we know of God—and also through the "glimpses" gained through the people who surround us.

Living Ready

In my teens, 20's and 30's, having a lasting life was nebulous. A tendency to form blood clots in my legs and abdomen brought me close to death numerous times. The good that came out of it includes learning to "live ready." Ready to die.

When death was knocking at my door, I had to deal with fear. For sure death is "the unknown." Psalm 23 became my main squeeze. Alongside that passage I memorized many others. 2 Timothy 1:7, was one that I repeated to myself most often, "For God has not given us a spirit of fear, but of power and of love and of a sound mind."

When I Googled "How many times are we told 'do not fear' in the Bible?" The first response found is remarkable, "It's been said that there are 365 'Fear Not' verses in the Bible—one for each day of the year." That may not be an exact count, but throughout Scripture fear is addressed as a common emotion that God wants to help us with by way of teaching us to trust Him.

Fortunately, I can look back with amazement at having now been given so many decades of life. After our children were raised and our "nest" became empty, I was able to finish my Master's Degree in Theology, along with Clinical Pastoral Education in a teaching hospital. Once Board certification in chaplaincy was gained, I was ready to follow a felt call of ministering to sick and dying people. My early life experiences prepared me for helping others who are facing grave uncertainties.

Most of us want certainty . . . which life does not afford us. In that regard, my work as a chaplain, in part, includes having thoughtful conversation with individuals helping them understand the importance of making "end of life" choices well in advance of death. It is vitally important to officially designate the person you want to speak for you, in the event there is a time when you cannot speak for yourself.

Many of us choose to put in place "Do Not Resuscitate (DNR)" and/or "Do Not Intubate (DNI)" orders. Seniors are often surprised to learn that unless this paperwork is in place, when hospitalized the medical team has no recourse than to do everything possible to keep them alive. Clearly, people can save themselves needless pain and perhaps suffering . . . and their loved ones a lot of angst by doing their "end of life" paperwork while they can.

Actor Gary Sinise wrote in his book, *Grateful American: A Journey from Self to Service,* a premise to which I adhere, "Each person on this planet is here for a purpose . . . That purpose is to care for other people and to help this world become a better place through service to others."

While working as a hospice chaplain, most of the patients I saw were given very little time to finish their life's journey. I help them look at what else they want in life. Part of that work includes looking at relationships, and when possible, making peace with those in which there is still pain. Forgiveness work allows for releasing the toxicity of resentment and bitterness, when this exists. In many cases, people welcome our praying together, which can make relational healing through forgiveness much easier. This often is the "one thing" that feels unfinished for the person who is getting ready to die, allowing for them to pass in peace.

The subject of, "What happens after death?" sometimes come up. As a chaplain, I see clearly that most seek answers and need love and acceptance; advice is best used with great caution. Listening is a skill all of us best learn, but for a chaplain this is imperative for truly being effective with patients. Sometimes people, when at death's door, will ask questions like, "How can I be ready to die?" Or, "I've not been religious. Help me know how to be ready to encounter God."

My response is, "Just talk to God. Tell Him about your struggle, wondering: 'is God real, or not?' Tell God you want to see Him and talk with Him in person. Ask, 'What do I need to do in order for that to happen?' Then listen."

I offer to help people pray, if this assistance is wanted. Helping them see what the Bible says about being assured of living on into eternal life, can be an important step—based on what the patient's desire becomes. For chaplains, helping people stay in their comfort zone while their bodily needs are met is the major goal, particularly within the hospital and rehabilitation settings.

Life is a mystery. Not one of us knows how much time we have on earth. A huge advantage comes through living ready for death. Ignoring the inevitable is not something to do right up to the end. We may not have consciousness at that point.

You may want to separate death from life, preferring not to think about it, but there is no doubt that death is a part of each person's life: many times ending with both beauty and grace.

"End of life" paperwork can be obtained from the Attorney General of the State in which you live. However, hospitals and hospices do customarily also have this paperwork.

"I'm going home!"

About two decades ago, I met James[5]. He was one of my first patients in hospice. After talking a few moments, he said, "I haven't been in church for many years. But, I was a Sunday school kid. Every Sunday, until I was a teenager, I was happy to go to church. Then there just wasn't a lot of thoughts going on about God."

Mostly our conversations were around his picturesque recounts of fishing as those trips were obviously the highlight of his life. I did enjoy hearing the stories but mostly savored how, at the very ending days of his life—with an IV in his arm—he was finding solace in those memories. Not at any point within my two home-hospice visits did James talk about his illness or dying.

This was a bit concerning. I had been trained to believe doctors always prepared a patient for entering hospice, telling them medical treatment would stop as it no longer held any promise for saving one's life. Hospice teams are experts at treating pain and fostering the highest level of comfort possible. Still, while with James, what seemed the right thing to do, was to just be there for him, letting him know I was enjoying what he was sharing. I could hear the rivers roar, in places . . . yet, also envision his fly fishing in the calmer, peaceful waters. He was that good with these stories.

Before my next scheduled visit to James' house, I got a call from his hospice nurse. She said, "James was hospitalized. We don't expect him to live beyond 48 to 72 hours."

Arriving at his hospital room, I figured James would want to talk about this part of his journey. But, no. After rousing a bit to speak, he said, "Let me tell you about the next fishing trip I'm going to make!"

---

[5] Names are changed to protect identities.

Again, I found listening was the only thing to do. Upon leaving, I did have some difficult feelings, telling myself, "The doctor has failed to tell this man the truth—he is dying!"

Early the next day I got a call from his wife, Sally. She said James had passed, then told me of their last moments, "I was sitting by his bedside while holding his hand. We were telling one another how much we love each other. Then James pulled his hand out of mine. I reached for it. But, James pulled it back. Suddenly he lifted both of his hands toward the ceiling and with a wide, wide smile, said with verve, 'I'm going home!'"

While officiating at his memorial service I shared this exceptional story of how Sally witnessed James at the moment of his being "beckoned in." Facing heaven, James found what "going home" truly means.

Children who go to Sunday school usually learn what it takes to have their names written in God's Book of Life. It might have been Daniel 12:1 that James' teacher had shared in class, indicating that everyone whose name is found written in the book will be rescued.

James' story makes me think of the Scripture in Proverbs 22:6, "Train up a child in the way he should go, and when he is old he will not depart from it."

For James, the seeds of truth about eternal life were planted in his soul at an early age, in Sunday school and perhaps by his parents. God gave him a long and enjoyable life—then, "beamed" him up.

A child may forget a prayer uttered long ago, but it is certain that God does not forget. James's "remembering" may have begun long before I arrived at his door, to sit a spell, and offer a prayer." He no doubt felt care and concern. Maybe the most precious gift we can give to one another is listening to each other's stories, truly hearing what is said.

Humans have an inner voice (or feeling) that prompts us—guides us toward right behavior and away from bad behavior. Abundant trouble comes when a person sears her or his conscience, by completely ignoring it, living only to promote one's self. This hardens the conscience and results in our lying to ourselves, saying, "It's OK to do it my way."

James's story is one of many indicating that people do at times, gain upfront evidence of what is ahead for believers after their time on earth, and then to remain, yet a while, knowing *heaven is for real.*[6]

[6]At healing-with-Joy.com, click "Near Death – N.D.E."

Flying low and flying high

Nature speaks, when we listen. Perhaps birds can be the most frequent bearers of messages. While in Idaho, walking along a hillside, I met with an Evening Grosbeak. The breeze blew the feathers of his head straight up as he lingered on a bush. But the remarkable moments came while watching this bird fly.

Although the pumping motion of his wings seemed adequate, the little creature was constantly sinking. Only short flights could be made from one tall weed to another in order to stay airborne.

Suffering from some unseen loss or wound, this bird let me get much closer than he otherwise would have allowed. But three feet was his limit, then he would plunge ahead. We traveled together like this for several hundred feet before he circled back into the subdivision and flew up to a doorway to find rest upon a light fixture. Vulnerable, without benefit of help, no doubt he would soon fall prey to a hungry predator, unless perchance a child with a B-B gun reached this wounded one first.

I thought of the similarity between the plight of the bird and that of suffering humans. When hurt, physically, mentally or emotionally, it is necessary to "fly low." Life must be taken in short distances; forced rest comes often. It is difficult and sometimes impossible to fend without help. There is a greater need to let others move in close—far closer than normally would be needed. Such state of life seems to invite "pot shots" from those who lack understanding, are prone to criticism or judgment: "Can't you fly a wee bit higher? Carry a little more of the load? Get squared away and not mope?"

Human intelligence can be a two-edged sword. The injured ones know what they have lost. There are memories of soaring high, times of having "wings on our feet," while tasting the pleasure that comes with providing for self and others. The sorrow of loss stings and constantly must be fielded.

Yet, this same gift of intelligence grants the power to supersede, to persevere—even transpose valleys into celestial realms unseen by the human eye. How can this be done? By acknowledging Christ, developing ears to hear His voice and the ability to respond in the spirit of the Psalmist:

The LORD *is* my shepherd; I shall not want . . . You prepare a table before me in the presence of my enemies; You anoint my head with oil; My cup runs over. Surely goodness and mercy shall follow me all the days of my life; and I will dwell in the house of the LORD forever," (Psalms 23:1-6).

Clearly, it is possible to see Christ's touch through the hands and hearts of others. While captured in a bed, while sick, one learns to lie still and know that God is there. Then when released again in the land of the living, there can be praise, exclamations of thanksgiving—for the gift of life resumed, even though it is not painless.

Human choice rules here. Some choose to draw inward, shrinking from loving help. Like Carl, a stroke victim and amputee who said, "I've learned two lessons in life: Mind your own business. And don't need anyone!" A felt gloom rose from his trap of bitterness. Obviously, his eyes were blinded; he could not see God all about him—nurses, doctors, therapists, dressings, medicine, plus a meal being wheeled in as he spoke. How I wanted to touch him with love, but like the little bird on the hillside Carl only felt safe in keeping his distance.

The subject of suffering has been addressed by many minds finer than mine. All of us have struggled with the questions of it. But, may each of us – sufferer and health-bearer alike—not fail to see the velvet glove of God present in every hour of pain or pleasure. May the able-bodied not "fly so high," or so fast as to fail hearing the words of a troubled heart. It only takes a moment to stroke a trembling hand. May we lay down the "B-B guns." For, that is Christ in that hospital bed, that wheelchair, in that quiet, lonely home. It is Christ behind that depressed or anxious face. Countless people wait for the sound of a ringing phone. Do we care?

The speed of life is a force to be reckoned with. There are slower lanes, which can be chosen, granting time to walk a mile with those who are there without choice. Is this our "road to Emmaus," where Christ is not so easily recognized, yet right there with us?

Smoke and Haze

When we see people with strength and courage, are they generally the ones we want to hang out with? Yes? No? Maybe? Or—it depends.

Reading Holy Writ opens our eyes to the fact God has a plan for the lives of all humans, one that creates strength and courage along with peace and joy. That plan is boldly stated—for those who find it. "Ask, and it will be given to you; seek, and you will find; knock and it will be opened to you," (Matthew 7:7).

The results of seeking "the plan" and following it includes getting a grip, while finding how greatly we are loved and treasured—even given the desires of our hearts. This promise is given to all who delight themselves in the Lord, one billions of people have found to be trustworthy. No "false news, here!"

But, we are human and even the best of the faithful have personal flaws to overcome. Life is about meeting challenges, one of which is moving through the smoke and haze of being imperfect. Throughout Scripture we are told over and over again that we are forgiven and that our hearts have been cleansed. "Come now let us reason together, says the Lord. Though your sins are like scarlet they shall be as white as snow; though they are red like crimson they shall be as wool," (Isaiah 1:18).

I belong to the "crowd of people" (2.5 billion Christians)[7] who trust in God and love the Bible, allowing God's Word to undergird and sustain us throughout the challenges of life.

---

[7]There are around 2.4 billion Christians in the world. Christianity has been the largest of all world religions for nearly two thousand years. A Christian seeks to follow what Jesus Christ called "the way." He made very clear in John 14:6, saying, "I am the way, the truth, and the life. No man comes to the father except through me." The word "religion" does not do justice to "the way" of Christians.

Having treasured "the Book" since a child of eight doesn't mean I was always grateful. Sometimes I was willful, making poor choices. However, I had the wherewithal to change my course. Only a dummy would fail to return to the Good Shepherd's fold after encountering the dark night caused by going one's own way.

I have "walked with the Lord since a child and have come to know that centering my life on Holy Writ creates a happy soul, one with purpose. A practice of memorizing Scripture has greatly enhanced my daily life, making it possible for these passages to come "alive" in a flash when help is needed.

Imagine having this mentally etched on one's soul: "Trust in the Lord and do good; dwell in the land, and feed on his faithfulness. Delight yourself also in the Lord, and He shall give you the desires of your heart. Commit your way to the Lord . . . (Psalm 37:3-5).

In this crowd of believers, to which I have belonged for the largest part of my life, we are referred to as "sheep." Why? Because we have a Shepherd who also becomes Lord of our lives. And he leads us "in green pastures" and "beside the still waters."

He restores our souls when there are times come during our stay on earth that find us feeling broken and in great need. Repeating Psalms 23 from memory can bring us back to that place of hope and trust wherein we live in peace, no matter what takes place. God takes the dark threads, weaving beautifully everything that happens within a believer's life.

With this Shepherd, we don't need to munch on the weeds. If ever we go out of bounds the shepherd searches us out. He finds His own—lifts us up from the brambles, carrying us home on his shoulder. Love overshadows us when we are lost. We come to see who we truly are, His Beloved.

There are trials enough to complete our training. The shepherd's guidance brings us to full maturity. He teaches us to be strong and courageous. We find peace in our hearts and joy in our souls. This gives us plenty of "highs" to serve us well. We have mountains to climb and rivers to cross, but Scripture lays out a path along which there are fortifying promises.

For one, "Count it all joy when you fall into various trials, knowing that the testing of your faith produces patience. But let patience do her perfect work, that you may be perfect and complete lacking nothing." Okay. Viola! Strength and courage are truly at work, here.

"The Book" tells us we are a "peculiar" people to those who are outside looking in. There will be a certain redolence about us. It is the aroma of our actions and attitudes, differing from what seems normal to people who are going it alone. For some, being around us may seem an experience of "smoke and haze." It is unknown territory for them. What we believe and talk about can seem challenging.

Amazingly enough, God has given us weak, little humans the right and the power to become children of God. It is not easy to see ourselves for who we are: people called to represent God to the world. And, often we do a poor job of it, as God is not finished with us, yet.

As the Lord's people, within His flock, we learn through our mistakes. With God's guidance we become strong, courageous and full of good cheer. We know where to go when we are hurting. We know who can heal us when we mess up.

This comes once we see the Lord, our Shepherd as having the answer to the longings of our souls. Our paths clear, as the wind of the Holy Spirit blows away our smoke and haze.

What bangs your shutters?

We want extraordinary things to happen in life. Sometimes it just takes a quick story or a joke to give us that chemical change we need. And, "yes" when our emotions move into that sweet range of joy, hope, even surprise (which excites us) our physiology changes.

The other day Bill Gates read one of my website blogs and responded. The surprise of that gave me a lift! My push to get through what was demanding to be done before the end of the day was forgotten while pondering his comment, "Very good feedback. Wondering what you think of its implication on society as a whole, though?"

My first thought was "right!" That's going to happen! Bill Gates, reading me? Yet, whoever this "Bill Gates" is, this is a person wanting to know my thoughts as regards the world at large. What an honor.

His observation included a reference to "things that can have global expansion, bringing frustration." He ended with "I'll be around soon to check out your response."

Hmmm. Now I'm thinking "maybe Bill Gates," as my website outreach has become rather wide. (I'm using Google translate, now, to understand messages coming from other countries.)

My follow-up thought was, OK, this guy cares. He ***might be*** Bill Gates, or an average guy who invests himself more than most in "what could make a better world."

Let's get real. It is not a person's name that gives him or her value and credibility. It's not even how much success has come to a person, or how much money is in a bank. Every person on the globe has innate value and deserves to be cared about and respected. Everybody has a story even if it doesn't rock the world digitally, or shake the boat we tie up by the lake.

Based on that truth, I decided to write a blog specific to Bill Gate's inquiry.

First, I need to decide which direction to go as I covered a lot in the column, titled, "My dream for the New Year," to which Mr. Gates responded. Was the point "pursuing patience by living in the moment" what he picked up on? Or was it, "valuing elderly folks in our society, listening to their stories?" Yet, could it be my reference to "being content with discovering pleasure in the commonplace?" No, I think this Bill Gates picked up on something from a poem by William Wordsworth, an English poet (1770-1850) that the website blog included:

"I heard a thousand blended notes, while in a grove I sat reclined, in that sweet mood when pleasant thoughts bring sad thoughts to the mind.

"To her fair works did Nature link the human soul that through me ran; and much it grieved my heart to think what man has made of man."

For sure it is great to enjoy the good things we make happen—to build families, and/or put our talents to work. Still, alongside that we must think also about what we have done to one another—and to our earth that shouts "Let's revisit this! Let's make amends."

In V*isions, Trips, and Crowded Rooms*, David Kessler wrote, "maturity is when you accept the fact that two contradictory ideas can exist together." His example was "community service can be a selfless and generous act, or it can be used for self-aggrandizement."

The most immanent contradiction is that this world is beautiful and "life is great." And, equally present is a truth that does create frustration (even fear): the entire ecosphere seems to be "going to hell in a hand basket," given all the shootings and the chaos here at home, as well as around the globe. "Wars and rumors of wars," is what Scripture prophecies for the "last days."

How can we maturely work with this?

The answers are in "the Book"—the Bible—for any who will look (and see), ponder and place trust. Two quick examples, Psalms 46:10, "Be still, and know that I am God . . . I will be exalted in the earth!" (Psalms 6:10).

And, Colossians 3:2, grants a directive for good mental health, "Set your mind on things above, not on things on the earth . . . . Verse 15 of that passage concludes, ". . . let the peace of God rule in your hearts to which also you were called in one body; and be thankful."

What God really wants of us is to, "love the Lord your God with all your heart and all your soul and your neighbor as yourself." This would be the ultimate in maturity. No frustration, here, Mr. Gates, for those advanced enough to see this truth and to live it out.

There is only one possibility in which Jesus' teachings could bring a frustration. That happens when people claim to follow Christ's teachings, yet fail to let God's inerrant assurance change their lives. Clearly, it is an individual's choice. Each can decide whether to follow his or her egocentric behaviors and philosophies allowing these to hold sway, or dedicate oneself to living by God's Word.

It is this belief in God and the Bible (His Word) that holds the power to change lives and bring the maturity we as human beings so badly need. These tenets, when lived out, serve to powerfully motivate us, creating the actions needed to eliminate what underlies human sufferings: hatred, poverty, tyranny and war (at home and globally.)

Truth be known—meaning if God's Word is fully lived out—we can have *peace on earth and goodwill for all.* But, 2nd Peter 3:3-4, does not extend hope for that, saying, "Scoffers will come in the last days, walking according to their own lusts and saying, 'Where is the promise of His coming?'" Verse 9, assures us, "The Lord is not slack concerning His promise, as some count slackness, but is longsuffering toward us, not willing that any should perish but that all should come to repentance." The ultimate in *peace and goodwill* certainly will be ours when Jesus Christ returns to the earth fulfilling His promise to come a second time. I, for sure, want to be living by His Word (the Bible) and ready for His coming.

Following are seasonal entries for your enjoyment

Christmas

What's new for Christmas?

"All I want for Christmas" is to stop hurting

We all are needy when it comes to this . . .

New Years

My dream for the New Year

All systems are 'GO!'

Hold it! There's one more thing!

Valentine's Day

Give yourself a Valentine

Easter

God's "major surgery" on a grandmother's heart

Why did they crucify him?

The crux of the cross

Good Fridays impact on life

Thanksgiving Day

On counting our blessings . . .

Labor Day

Parents say the darndest things!

What's new for Christmas?

What's new for this Christmas? Perhaps a season where funds are low and life seems "topsy-turvy"? And, if so, should we despair, and indulge in self-pity? Or, can we feel challenged to experience the true meaning of Christmas by simply scattering some kindness to others?

Today, I saw such an act at the post office drive-through letter station. The wind blew an envelope out of one of the over-filled letter drops. A man ran, chasing the envelope, so he could re-deposit it for someone who was no doubt a stranger. A "Merry Christmas" message for another will now arrive.

We can get into the buying "hoop-la," where it seems all about shopping and frantic antics as we race against the clock with some anxiety about December 25 "getting so close." Puzzling over what to buy—and who we might be forgetting—we buck the traffic. Plus the crowds can just plain wear us out! With time stretching taut as a rubber band, it is easy to think something might snap and maybe that something could be you, or me!

All of this is part of the holiday scene in most American homes. But let's think for a moment about how we might find and extend to others what Christ, in coming to this world, meant to bring. Light where there is darkness. Empathy where there is loneliness . . . and tender hearted prayerfulness for the many who are teetering on the edge of survival.

The gospel is most challenging. Jesus spoke of bringing the poor into our homes. And, it is not always monetary poverty that people are dealing with. There is social poverty—and the physical poverty that poor health can bring. We celebrate with gifts, yes. Yet a gift of time can be greater, by far, than anything that might be purchased, like an evening's visit, a Sunday call, a note which is unexpected. Could there be a neighbor, friend or distant relative that we might consider extending our Christmas to, someone we have not thought of for a long stretch of time?

But when it all comes down to facts, Christmas comes to us because of Christ. He is the true and lasting reason for celebrating. Most of us have received countless gifts in life. Yet, have we truly accepted the gift of His personhood? Having a cognitive knowledge of God is far different than having the experience of the One (Jesus) who said, "I am the light of the world. He who follows Me shall not walk in darkness, but have the light of life," (John 8:12). So, we celebrate Christmas with lights all over the place. But, do we miss finding "*the light of life*" through reaching for His presence—and His love—that can change us . . . make us all we were meant to be?

We soon will be meeting Christ in the manger as we recall *the greatest happenstance the world has experienced—one* that has changed billions of lives. It will be no time at all before we "meet Him," again, at Lent in the story of the cross. But it is the daily experiencing of Jesus Christ, knowing Him on an intimate basis that changes and fills our lives with light. Clearly, He came to this earth, not because God the Father demanded or expected this of Him, but because of His love for us. We, the people, are His treasure. We bring our lives to Him—gifts better than frankincense, myrrh and gold.

So, Christmas comes annually as an opportunity for some to discover Christ. Others, will "miss it," breeze by it, letting commercialism rule. Meanwhile, believers worship Christ as our thoughts are foremost of Him. For over two thousand years, believers have found Jesus Christ to be the greatest of all treasures. While pondering the majesty of Jesus lying in a manager, we find him vitally alive in our hearts. Seeking, wherever possible, to carry His light and love into every nook and corner of the world that He has entrusted to us. This is our gift back to Him.

So, "What's new for Christmas?" Perhaps, for some, it will be finding the majesty of Christ for the first time.

“All I want for Christmas” is to stop hurting

When the woman who said this told her story I understood. Yes. I could understand her statement of her foremost “want,” but wasn’t ready for what she said next, “Where’s Jesus when we hurt?

Her life pain was increased by the loss of her husband—now Christmas is around the corner. Countless people are suffering similarly. Having presents under the trees may not be the most concerning factor for many this year. So where is Jesus? And, what is He doing about this?

Following Jesus’ death and resurrection, the apostle Paul assured us Jesus is “at the right hand of God, who indeed is interceding for us,” (Romans 8: 34). Intercessory prayer for one another is a great thing, but imagine the Lord Jesus Christ pulling for us as we tackle our problems and struggles in life—even those that are self-inflicted by our poor decisions that we make without having prayed for guidance.

He alone holds power to lead us to green pastures and still waters. He alone can turn all that happens to good. Even our hardest of happenstances are teachers. We gain patience, as we hang in there and master them! And, it is patience that makes us “complete, lacking nothing,” (See James 1:2).

Our trials find us trusting God more and more fully. We become the hurdlers, leaping above the obstacles facing us. Our growing faith motors us, while also comforting us during the hardest moments. Kneeling, praying and asking for discernment is how we get through it when we hurt so much we can hardly bear it . . . and settles us when we seek to comprehend.

Methods many use to escape life’s difficulties, like drinking to gain escape, are by far ineffective. This is true, too, of using pills to surmount the throes of life. These cannot take a person high enough to satisfy the cravings developed. Consequently, many are dying through overdoses while trying to reach an ultimate "high" once again.

Billions of people over the past 2,000 years have found through Scripture that Jesus is the only steadfast answer. And, as the Apostle John assures us, Jesus did not just come at Christmas. No. At the earth's beginning, "He was in the world, and the world was made through Him, and the world did not know Him, (John 1:10)."

John knew Christ as "the Word." "In the beginning was the Word, and the Word was with God, and the Word was God. He was in the beginning with God. All things were made through Him, and without Him nothing was made that was made. In Him was life, and the life was the light of men. And the light shines in the darkness, and the darkness did not comprehend it," (John 1:1-5).

We celebrate December 25, with many lights—in remembrance of when Jesus came to us, birthed here on earth in person, to live among us as a human being in a body of flesh like our own. Why? So He could look us in the face as humans, experience what we experience. He chose this setting alone in which to teach us about the Father's love for us and about a kingdom *that is ours while here*. Romans 14:17, makes it clear God's kingdom is one of "righteousness, peace and joy in the Holy Spirit."

He also leads us to be His hand and feet on the earth. Think of His love that flows at places like food banks where people volunteer their time and their money while doing their best to assure families are fed. It is an awesome time!

Right here in the midst of earthly realms, there is this great and mighty kingdom of goodness ("Godness"). Jesus prayed to His Father for us, "I have given them Your word; and the world has hated them because they are not of the world, just as I am not of the world. I do not pray that You should take them out of the world, but that You should keep them from the evil one. They are not of the world, just as I am not of the world," (John 17:14-16).

Father God allowed him to come here, to die for us and pave the way for our having eternal life once we leave this earth. God knows we are sinful—and He cannot look at sin. When He sent His son to be with us

God was extending His nature to us . . . making it possible for us to take on His very own nature.

Our nature is naturally a "fallen nature." All humans are prone to follow it. God loves us so much that He sent His only begotten son to be a surrogate for us. Jesus' purpose was many faceted, yet majorly to die for us. He carried our sins as the Roman soldiers crucified Him. From there on, we have only to trust, knowing our sins are covered by the Savior's blood. His blood is our covering. "There is therefore now no more condemnation for those who are in Christ Jesus, who do not walk according to the flesh, but according to the Spirit," (Romans 8:1).

As Christmas approaches, the greatest thing a person can do in life is to recognize the truth of who Jesus is, and to know He has paved a way for us to be sin-free as we believe in His name and put our trust in Him. This is "the way" we come to relying on the help of His Holy Spirit day-by-day. In this way, Jesus is with us now, He said, He would always be with us," *even* unto the end of the world." (See the Great Commission below.)

So, how do we have a "Merry Christmas" in the midst of the troubles we face that life presents daily? The answer is simple, come to know who Jesus is—besides the one we remember at "Christmas." Reading the Gospels (the "Good News") allows us to see that Jesus is here—able to live in our hearts, doing through us what can relieve the pain of others. How? As the Lord's Holy Spirit nourishes us, our spirits are uplifted, fortified and enabled. Who can find a greater "merriment" than this?

Christmas holds more than a celebration of Jesus' birthday. The crux of all that happened within His life is recorded for us in Matthew 28:16-20. For, after He was crucified and before His returning to the Father in heaven, Jesus' last words carried a commission:

"And Jesus came and spoke to them, saying, "All authority has been given to Me in heaven and on earth. Go therefore and make disciples of all the nations, baptizing them in the name of the Father and of the Son and of the Holy Spirit, teaching them to observe all things that I have commanded you; and lo, I am with you always, *even* to the end of the age. ′Amen"

We are all needy when it comes to this . . .

Years ago while driving down the road in my vintage wine-colored Monte Carlo—favorite of all my cars—I realized the meaning of "unconditional love." At the time, I had been married to my husband Gary for 30 years. He is not one who easily says, "I love you." Yet, he is one who shows it throughout every avenue of our lives.

As a child, my parents' love was never spoken—yet shown through the ways family needs were provided: the roof over head, food on the table, clothing and supplies for school. Yet, I did not hear, "I love you" from parents striving to make ends meet. Instead, I learned I had "better behave." The importance of gaining my parent's good pleasure became eminently important to me. So, doing all possible to gain it, was my childhood quest. The message, "Love will always be here for you," was not perceived by me. No. The message that stuck was all about chores, being smart—getting good grades--and behaving. "You had better not mess up!" was the major message.

I did grow into loving, more than fearing my parents as an adult. But, as a kid, I held more fear of them than any other emotion. Maybe this is normal for a lot of people. Or, maybe most children are hugged daily and told, "I love you." We only know our own experience.

Finding love of any kind in life's journey is the highest of all quests, finding unconditional love is a pinnacle that I dare to say few truly reach.

Our early experiences within childhood, are brought into our marriages. In my first marriage at age 17, right out of high school, the honeymoon was short. It was however, a brief experience of being adored. Whoa. That was a first. Yet, within only a number of days, I knew the hand of authority was back. The old fear of not being enough or good enough was fully felt. This lasted eight years . . . eight years of figuring out that living in constant fear was no way to live. So, the only healthy choice was to leave. The soul ripping process of divorce became inevitable for the sake of safety and sanity.

Four years later, I started dating Gary, I knew he was different from any one I had ever met, yet my early programming was so linked to "pleasing" others that I had an unspoken fear of "when is the heavy hand going to come down on my back." Yet, that never happened. Still, that inner angst was there… expecting the worst. So, that day after 30 years of marriage, while driving down the road, I realized something about God that was actually happening in my life: unconditional love! Who knew it existed—and is real? Finding it in a human form through Gary, allowed me to comprehend the magnanimous love that He has for us. I remember the day so clearly, while driving, when the realization came: Gary only saw me as good. My flaws, well—flaws happen. He looked beyond those. Then, I remembered something my father said after having a dream.

Dad experienced a scar-filled childhood. He, too, feared his father throughout life and was sure "that guy" would not be in heaven. Although, during his later years my grandfather had changed and was in church every Sunday.

As my father was nearing death he shared a dream in which his mother and father were walking arm-in-arm into a huge banquet room—in heaven. He knew it was heaven, but he couldn't believe his Dad was there. Then, within the dream Dad heard these words, "I only see the good." Voila! Here is love—unconditional love. And, this is the message God has for us.

And, this is the truest and greatest gift of Christmas. God looked past the sin, the brokenness of this world, and sent His Son to save us from ourselves. Left alone, there would be no eternity with God for any one of us. But, Jesus came to us, knowing He would shed His blood to cover the tab for our "miss-steppings," and all the grossness that comes through the human race's self-importance and self-adoration. Now, through Him, God sees "price paid" as He cherishes His children. It is the all-pervading, all accepting love of God that has provided this truth for God's children: He only sees the good!

Here is an amazing truth from John 1:5, 12, "The light shines in the darkness, and the darkness did not comprehend it." And. verse 12 says,

"But as many as received Him, to them He gave the right to become children of God, to those who believe in His name."

What a difference it makes to grasp this truth. For, it is the truth of God's unconditional love that empowers and impassions those He calls—and we know when that call comes!

My dream for the New Year

Thoughts of Hazel, one of my heroes, comes to mind. She had her 89th birthday soon after our meeting. Still chewing on life, as if a piece of gristle, Hazel could put many to flight with her questions and ideas. It did not take long to learn the secret of this woman's personal agility and mental acumen, as Hazel's abilities were daily in demand. Her life is pledged to the care of a physically challenged daughter, then 56. This octogenarian is hot on the trail of what many, much younger, folks have perhaps not even thought about: the pursuit of patience needed for moment-to-moment endurance. She was extraordinary.

Years back, Jessica Savitch interviewed Whoopi Goldberg on television. Whoopi told of her mother referring to her as "extra ordinary," when she was a child. Whoopi said, "I used to think she meant extraordinary. But, all the time she just meant 'extra ordinary.'" Whoopi believed she could do extraordinary things. So, she has! Her keen ability to impersonate common people and ordinary events, while bringing humor to the mundane has enriched many lives. Historically, Whoopi has shared her extraordinary ability to shed delightful color on the simplicity and silliness of our everyday selves.

Clearly, the "extra ordinary" person Whoopi's mother spoke of could best describe Hazel, my new found hero. She has not experienced fame, yet "extraordinary" describes Hazel well, as her dedication is carried with such grace and fortitude as to be challenging for some and encouraging for others.

So often we go through life longing for extraordinary experiences, eagerly awaiting the exceptional, the remarkable to take place. When all the time the real joy of living is found in being content with and discovering pleasure in the commonplace—in the present moment, especially while listening to the stories of others.

Extraordinary happenings of life, which always come, bring great surprise along with that occasional bit of rapture so good for the soul. However, if we are constantly on the hunt for the "peaks," of finding what is superbly uncommon—the experiences that can titillate or otherwise thrill—then ordinary happenstances, like hearing the stories of another's life, could just seem dull.

For sure, the conversation of a person who has traversed the earth for 7-9 decades can take a little more time and perhaps more patience while listening. Being in a hurry, may mean wisdom is lost. A prevalent *"On with the action"* mode of being is easy to slip into.

Fascinated by the unusual, all sorts of memorabilia entice us. We collect stamps, papers, dolls, books, bottles and old coins—antiques of every sort. And, what happens to people who have accumulated great age? Those seen as "spent" are warehoused far too often; as if human souls can be pushed into "attics" until "collected" by someone who stumbles onto the truth of their value . . . long after the person's demise. They then may exclaim, "Hey, this person had it together!" Yes, surely some must live out the last months and sometimes even years of their lives in care centers. But must they be deserted mentally and emotionally?

The following segment of a poem by William Wordsworth, the English poet (of 1770-1850), speaks of this:

"I heard a thousand blended notes,

While in a grove I sat reclined,

In that sweet mood when pleasant thoughts

Bring sad thoughts to the mind.

To her fair works did Nature link

The human soul that through me ran;

And much it grieved my heart to think

What man has made of man."

There seems to be a bit of "bareness" as people reach their later years. But, what if we determine to affirm the elderly—the "antique people" and seek out their stories. Envision our ability to validate them in such ways as they feel there is still beauty and purpose in being here.

My dream for this year is for growth in the ability to enjoy the ordinary, while also honing in on the stories of my fellow globe-trotters. I want to listen better and be able to perceive their richness, solidity and wisdom. It is similar to how those of us who live in the Arizona desert develop a keen ability to see past barrenness, as our eyes are ever finding the beauty that is there for those who have the "eyes to see it."

The Bible holds great hope. Psalm 92:12-14, shows people "in old age" as "still bearing fruit . . . fresh and flourishing, declaring their faith in the Lord."

Way to go!

All systems are 'GO!'

Or, not?

On New Year's Eve, someone asked, "What is the difference between a resolution and a goal?" After thumbing through a dictionary, I found a "resolution" means to have "a firm determination to do something," while a "goal" is "the purpose toward which an endeavor is directed."

Most of us have less than a positive attitude toward New Year's resolutions. Yet, although challenging, are they not tremendous benefits to us? Yes. They can be the impetus by which we reach our goals. They are stimulants for our systems which otherwise can get sluggish.

So, failed resolutions, although made sincerely, are not the problem. We are. For, upon sensing that we will not be able to hit our mark, we start feeling bad about ourselves, seeing this as certain failure, rather than an "alert light," indicating a change is necessary in order to stay on target. Like a rocket reaching for its orbit we, too, will fall short if there is inadequate combustion (determination and faith) behind our thrust.

For sure, without commitment to go all the way with resolutions they fail. It takes being fully committed to our commitments, in order to launch the change we want.

Within spiritual counseling, I often ask people, "If you could do anything in the world you wanted, no holds barred, what would it be?" Most people can quickly answer, but their answers almost never match what they are currently doing.

When I ask them what stands in their way, an outstanding truth is always revealed. Dreams are only planted in the heart when the possibility of it being reached exists. It may take some significant planning—and sometimes even years of schooling, but there is always a way to stay on course, when one's desire is strong enough.

Could it be that many of us move through time just letting life happen to us? Have we never truly reached deep enough to find out what we really want? Without believing in ourselves, we cannot move forward in our gifts in such a way as to bring glory to God to the extent this truly can happen.

The greatest problem for most of us is that we lack the ability to hear God and to choose to follow His lead. A determination to allow Him to lead our lives is powerful. And, God will give us the faith and the strength needed to put aside our doubts and choose to stay on course with righteous goals. Sure, most of us lack self-confidence, but a growing faith can kick that to the curb. God will do the work through us when we believe He is in the recipe.

What if we truly believe that we are Sons and Daughters of God, "created in the image of God"—the one who has given us our very breath? One who is able to place a dream in each heart, with gifts and talents enough to match it? The great Father of heaven looks about the earth with love, hoping to find His people happy, enjoying the world He has made. In many cases, we haven't dared to discover the totality of our gifts.

Someone once said, "Nothing is work unless you would rather be doing something else." True. Yet some parts of every activity are less enjoyable, so we will always have work to do. How much greater this world would be if every one of us could work mostly toward what we truly want to take place through us while here on Planet Earth.

God has created us with the capacity to dream, so undoubtedly He will be there for us as we move toward fulfilling those dreams. The issues that keep us from embracing the longings of our hearts come from self-doubt, a lack of trust that God can—and will—help us make commitments and reach our goals.

Is there any good reason why we cannot state what the Apostle Paul said, "I can do all things through Christ who strengthens me" (Philippians 4:13). Believing this on a daily basis will greatly increase confidence and make it possible to maximize our abilities.

Surely we will always be happiest when we are in some way giving of ourselves. It is how God made us—loving to create, loving to help another. It is the key to "the ignition" of happiness.

So, let's consider a New Year's challenge before January is over. Let's request God's help in checking out "the inner blueprint," asking "Am I doing what I truly want to do?" Then, if not, "What is stopping me?"

And let's go for it! It's not too late.

Hold it! There's one more thing!

So, now you have taken the challenge. You have answered the question, "If I could do anything in the world I wanted – no holds barred – what would it be?" Now, there's one more thing . . .

After deciding what we want to achieve in life, plans are formulated by which to start. Yet, there is one more step, at least for the believer. That is to ask for God's help in answering another question: "In the event I follow this course, will the reaching of my goal bring me into a closer relationship with God—or will doing so put distance between us?"

The answers to these questions will tell us a lot. Yes, God does "delight in our recipe," as long as we are delighting in Him. But, human tendency being what it is, we are apt to run about like little gods attempting to be in control of our plan, every single detail of it.

In looking back over my life, I see several goals met thus far, encompassing years of hard work. Some of these years were spent simply trying to discover what worked for me—what would satisfy my tremendous need to produce and achieve. God, patient as He is, held steady. My guess is that He would have preferred to spare me some of the agonies, but He respected me enough to let me learn.

There were the years as a sales manager. But top sales, trophies, awards (such as jewelry, trips, etc.) did not bring any lasting satisfaction. After this, four years of selling real estate and making a considerable amount of money also didn't feel truly rewarding. Then, came my Jonah years, in which I found the "belly of the whale" to be the worst place of all.

It was while in a hospital bed facing eternity that I saw what God was saying. "You're killing yourself!" As the months and even years of pain, disability, and extreme fatigue passed, I learned to listen. And, guess what: God was not asking me to knock myself out like that! No, He was inviting me to believe that the very thing I had always wanted to do was exactly right.

In the early years, writing poetry, letters and even simple thoughts brought a great sense of wellbeing. This writing, allowed an awareness of having linked myself with what was most important in life: learning to seek God's will while here in the land of the living. But I could never show these works to others. It felt as if my soul was lying on those pages. I dared not risk rejection. So, my writings remained, quietly, in a dresser drawer.

Then, while lying on sheets starched so hard they hurt, I began to realize a couple of important truths. There is precious little relevance in caring what people think. And, spending a lifetime of trying to prove one's worth can greatly shorten the duration of time on earth. So I vowed, "God, if you will let me live, I will write." What I meant is that I would write and share it with others.

Scripture shows us something interesting about why we were created. We were created to fellowship with God (be companions), and to "make him proud" (meaning to bring Him glory as Scripture puts it). And, He is out to help us do it! Our part is to overcome the fears and let go elements of pride that might be laced within the desire to bring some distinction to ourselves.

There is no sin in God; His kind of "pride" is worlds away from ours. His delighting in us enriches everyone. Our kind of pride seeks to enrich ourselves.

So, whatever it is that lies deep inside you, God is in it. He beckons each one of us to believe "we can do all things through Christ who strengthens me," (Philippians 4:13).

Give yourself a Valentine

There seems to be a powerful inner aversion to loving and appreciating ourselves, at least for many of us.

We wrap ourselves up in "Almighty Work" with goals for owning lovely homes, impressive cars, garments of every shape and color. This is all well and good, as long as the work itself and what we are able to produce through it, are not perceived to be the measure of our worth.

True celebration of what could offer heartfelt, memorable moments is robbed of its glory, as most often work wins out. Who has not felt an edge of guilt while sitting with a treasured book? After all, the yard needs work and floors beg cleaning.

Yet, life can become monotonous if we don't recognize the importance of making sure there is time to enjoy and savor the fruits of our labors—alongside clocking in at work, plus cleaning pots and pans and doing the laundry, while training energized children!

Always, there will be the inevitable surprises of life. Having a balanced life makes us better prepared for these when they come.

Loving ourselves means taking time out to simply enjoy the gift of human "beingness." Like taking an hour to read a novel—or even 15 minutes to simply think about good memories . . . playing with the children, or the dog . . . take a walk or run through the park. . . have a meaningful conversation . . . or write a loving letter to a close friend. These are a few poignant ways for reviving the spirit. It just takes loving oneself enough to grant these little leisures.

Then, what of the Sabbath day of rest we are called to set aside for restful wholeness? Have you ever noticed how many promises are extended for those who obey this Biblical commandment? It seems to be a direct criterion for good health and happiness, yet so often is ignored. We wonder why our hearts skip beats, flutter amiss or give up early. Could it be that we are failing to give ourselves essential time for restoration?

Charles E. Cowman, author of the devotional titled *Streams in the Desert*, wrote, "There is no music in the rest, but there is the *making* of music in the rest." What would it be like if instruments in the orchestra sounded with every beat? No doubt discomfort or anxiety would see us walking out before the performance ends.

Could it be prideful attitudes, thinking we are indestructible and indispensable, or lack of trust in the "Conductor" that keeps us from following undisputable directives? Or, a rebellious attitude . . . "I'll play it my way."

God loved us so much He gave commands to keep us from running amok. It is actually good self-love when we keep them. However, life without respect for God's directives brings brokenness, deficits, regrets and guilt! We all are in the same drum kettle. We want to make beautiful music with our lives. Doing so means we must practice good self-care by taking time to listen for what is taking place in our souls.

Being one's own best friend means we won't believe the worst about ourselves just because it is easiest. Instead we will weed out those harsh, chastising, guilt-ridden messages that can be prevalent—the negative self-talk—and speak up for our own solid goodness. After all, we are children of God. And, "God don't make junk," as one fine author states it.

It is when we truly begin to get a sense of our own goodness, instead of becoming self-centered (as is easily feared) that love moves outward, evidenced by a strengthened capacity for more earnestly caring about others and even the whole world.

I will never forget a day while driving down McCullock Avenue, here in Lake Havasu, when a thought made a quantum leap into my consciousness. In a momentary awakening, the usual "me first" attitude is replaced by an indescribable sense of oneness. For several moments it seems we all are moving to the beat of One Heart.

I was flooded with the deepest sense of caring never experienced before--an intense desire for all of us to arrive on time, whatever the place or the cause, filled my thoughts. Since then, a truth is becoming apparent: The more I love myself, the more capacity there is to love others. Was Jesus trying to tell us this when He said, "Love your neighbor as yourself?"

What if we do the ultimate, by becoming more in tune with "the Director," intent on following what He called "the first command, "you shall love the Lord our God with all your heart, with all your soul, with all your mind, and with all your strength," Mark 12:30. A love and appreciation of self (and others) could flow, even on McCulloch! Happy Valentine's Day.

God's 'major surgery' on a Grandmother's heart

As Easter approaches, so also does Bethany's birthday. Thirty-three years ago, this "little teacher" came into my family. Just prior to her birth a rather strange experience occurred.

With very few exceptions, everything I purchased over several weeks seemed flawed in some way. Back to stores I go, over and over, toting my purchases where patient salesclerks make exchanges. This happened enough that I decide to pray, "God, this is strange. Is there message I am supposed to be "getting?"

What was to come was something I could not easily accept. I was soon to face up to my silly perfectionism.

After three sons and three grandsons, our long awaited granddaughter was born. There could not have been a more proud or happier heart than mine. All those precious dreams were about to come true in this *perfect* little granddaughter for whom I had waited so long!

Then came the call, a few hours after her birth, "Mom, pray for the baby. They think she has Down's syndrome."

I was alone at home when Ted called, which was good. During the next couple of hours, God had "major surgery" to do on this grandmother's heart. I was stumbling all over what this would mean.

Then the trip to the hospital where Bethany is placed in my arms. All that armor against "imperfections" was pierced by a tiny hand. Sleepy little fingers . . . what healing they hold. In those moments, all is well.

Sure, pondering continued as I behold this newest member of our family. And, there are fears. But what truly amazes me is how right up to the moment of embrace I wanted to change her. Then the essence of her "beingness" reaches out bringing stillness to my soul. I recall, what inspired the Psalmist: *"Be still and know that I am God."*

Several days later, when the medical testing came back positive we were all fairly ready for it. Still, my emotions did some flip-flops. I was concerned as to what life would hold for her. My emotions would bounce between anger, denial and acceptance. Fortunately, somewhere along life's way I learned the uselessness of trying to bargain with God, so I skipped that one.

Many prayers were said for strength and understanding as our entire family makes adjustments. Praise and thanksgiving were also offered knowing Bethany has love and acceptance in the home God has placed her.

My son, like his mother, grapples with many a thought, many a feeling—yet, he comes through. It is plain to see he will be exceedingly caring and protective of this little one.

Bethany, meaning "house of God" seems to exude love. Everyone clamors for their turn to hold her—right down to her two-year-old brother. We cannot understand God's ways. His truth reaches deep, "For My thoughts are not your thoughts, nor are your ways my ways," says the Lord. For as the heavens are higher than the earth, so are My ways higher than your ways, and My thoughts than your thoughts," (Isaiah 55:8-9).

It is easy to see Him in Bethany, our "little one who needs a friend to live," is how John Vanier portrays the needs of children at L'Arche.

Wonder of wonders, each heart in this family has stretched like rubber bands. Now, with enlarged capacity, we can truly receive heaven's great message … one of life, and of love.

It is impossible to know what is ahead. But one thing is sure. Bethany is perfectly ours. She is God's extraordinary gift to an ordinary family. Only eternity will reveal her work.

People call it a "birth defect." Although surely having passed through God's Hand before reaching us, this circumstance is sanctified, bringing with it opportunities to embrace suffering with love. Bethany, one who is unable to speak, has underscored this message.

Peace and acceptance comes in remembering, “Trust in the Lord with all your heart, and lean not on your own understanding; in all your ways acknowledge Him, and He shall direct your paths” (Proverbs 3:5-6).

Within hardships, adjustments and unanswerable questions, it is how we handle these that tell whether or not we are living in faith . . . truly able to “be Christ’s presence” to one another. It is so easy to fool ourselves.

For me, pride can easily slip in, at points, insisting everything needs to be perfect. Of course being disappointed in myself follows, as I cannot be perfect. Humility comes when I pray to God, “In the midst of all this imperfection I will ever seek Your grace for the perfecting of my faith.”

The events of life bring attitudinal changes—if we are “listening.”

Fortunately, God is unlike the local merchant. He is more interested in perfecting character—than in having “satisfied customers.”

‘Happy birthday, Bethany”—and “many more.”

It is a day in which to rejoice.

Why did they crucify Him?

Have you ever wondered why Jesus, who went about healing and giving hope to the multitudes, became hated and hung—nailed to a cross? What is in human nature that can produce such heinous behavior?
Several years ago, I attended a workshop where in small groups we discussed what Christ's life was all about. In conclusion of our studies, we all were sure jealousy was what took Him to the cross.

Of course, the powers of both political and religious factions had strategies in place. Scripture depicts jealousy and fear spreading like wildfire. But it also makes it clear that God was at work unfolding His eternal plan for our salvation from our sins. It was all about Jesus' love for us, as He became "God's sacrificial lamb." The blood of God's son would henceforth cover our sins.

A woman, who was gifted from birth with a beautiful voice, sat at my table at the workshop. Knowing I was there, covering the event for the press, she leaned forward and said, "If you are going to write something, write about jealousy." Then she told her story.

In her early years of school, a teacher harshly criticized her voice, telling her she could not carry a tune. By high school, it was a different story. There her music teacher encouraged her to develop her voice as surely she had a "marketable product."

This woman grew up using her gift in her church, longing to honor only her Lord. In time, invitations carried her ability beyond the church to weddings, funerals, and other occasions. Always she sang sacred songs. She told of the pain that had come through cruel remarks that had caused her to question her gift as she was belittled—undermined in the little ways . . . and sometimes met with outright meanness.

This beautiful wounded one, who, in addition, was graced with humility, kept on singing, albeit often over sets of envious eyes. It took all the courage she could muster to keep standing before crowds, ministering in the way she felt called.

In a way, Jesus had a song. He, too, sang it in his own hometown. The power and the wisdom of His words were undeniable, but there, on His own turf, He had little if any respect. Jealousy was aroused when He began healing people. Scripture says, "They took offense at Him." How dare he, a local carpenter, move from that mold? They did not want to believe. So, they hardened their hearts against him and His miracles.

Eventually, a company of 12 men, deciding the presence and power of God was in Jesus, chose to walk with Him. They, too, sacrificed their lives for extending Christ's teachings.

His song was heard and revered all along the paths He trod. Gaining momentum, it reached its crescendo on a cruel cross. His was a song picked up by followers and carried across the centuries, today still capturing hearts.

Yes, time and time again we meet with truth. Anyone who sings the song of Christ, the Great Troubadour must also carry a cross. For, rivalry rests uneasily, like a cocklebur, at the core of the human soul. That desire to be equal to or better than the other serves to breed divisions, envy and fear.

Christ bequeathed us the power to die to these desires. Still, we may at times feel inept when someone close to us steps forward and shows signs of greatness. Those twinges of discomfort are about fear of being left behind—fear of relationships never being the same again. Resounding again and again the tune of our need to curb, change and exert control. Sometimes it is about wanting the same kind of appreciation and praise, yet not being willing to find one's own specialness, or giftedness.

Imagine how different the world would be if each one within it could be dedicated to encouraging others, helping them discover, develop and refine their area of greatness, that realm in which their "songs" could best be sung and heard.

Do you suppose there will be a time, after which we all have passed over into eternal realms, when each of us will be surprised at who we walked with? No doubt Jesus will be drying some tears as we fully realize our behaviors that actually suppressed or even oppressed another. A beautiful passage of Scripture shows Jesus wiping our tears away. His love is greater than our wrongs.

People of all the many ages across time keep repeating same behaviors. For instance, if Jesus were to step forward today from the midst of one of our cities under the guise, of say, a welder proclaiming a message that challenged ways we are comfortable with, do you think things would be much different than it was for Jesus, a carpenter in Galilee?

Today's critics and skeptics would no doubt make His work quite hard. Curious, yet castigating crowds would play their part. Would he again be likely to search out humble men and women, maybe blue collar workers, to be His disciples? Surely His miracles would be questioned, or refuted. Perhaps His greatest pain of all would come from needing to break away from people with whom He held close ties. He would know, while heading down the freeway to follow His call, that human nature hasn't changed.

But, thanks be to God for the cross, followed by His resurrection! The culmination of Jesus' life grants us the power to be different from the throngs who stood watching on that long day at Golgotha, as they witnessed Him breathe His last breath.

For many of us, His last words were vibrantly full of love, "Father, forgive them, for they do not know what they do," (Luke 23:34).

"For God so loved the world that He gave His only begotten Son, that whoever believes in Him should not perish but have everlasting life. For God did not send His Son into the world to condemn the world, but that the world through Him might be saved," (John 3:16-17).

Each one of us decides whether or not to believe that kind of love exists for us. The choice to believe, or not to believe, is ours.

The Crux of the cross

I was a high school student the day I met Jaylyn, a young woman that I will remember forever. I only encountered this person on one occasion. The three of us who were visiting had less than an hour with Jaylyn that day, yet, she became an unforgettable person in my life. She survived a fire seven years before we met her. I admit being taken back inwardly at first glance. Her scaring was immense. Then I saw her Bible.

I have loved my Bible from childhood, but never before had I seen one so worn. How could this book be so enlarged and seemingly frayed? Obviously, from years of being her mainstay. She must have lived within those pages that were roughed up from being so very well read.

From the moment of seeing this book, it stood fast in my mind as having been a monumental force and strength in her life. Jaylyn had found God's great love, His strength, comfort and solace.

Self-sufficiency can keep us from the Bible. Yet, for a person who recognizes their need of God and faith, the Bible becomes the greatest of all sources for courage, tenacity and strength. What made Jaylyn different, besides the scars? How could she exude such grace and peace to us, three teenagers who came to visit? Seeing her Bible was enough. We knew she had found Christ.

That day while being in her home, I could not know how deep and wide her influence would become for me. In a very short time--in less than two years--I would be enduring emboli as they struck my heart and lungs. Hoping and praying to stay alive, the Bible became my fortress, day and night. I came to more fully lean on the One around which Scripture swirls. Here is what the Bible reveals as the crux of the cross:

Jesus is "the true Light which gives light to every man coming into the world. He was in the world, and the world was made through Him, and the world did not know Him. He came to His own, and His own did not receive Him," (John 1:9).

John, a disciple of our Lord reveals Jesus as "the Word"—a truth that hold infinite power. In the first verse of his writing John helps us see what this statement means:

"In the beginning was the Word, and the Word was with God, and the Word was God. He was in the beginning with God. All things were made through Him, and without Him nothing was made that was made."

In verse 5, more is explained, "In Him was life, and the life was the light of men. And the light shines in the darkness and the darkness did not comprehend it."

The Lord came to save us from our sins, but also to teach us how God wants us to live. While here on earth, His message was received exceedingly well at first, based too, on the miracles He performed. But because of Jesus' growing influence, those who despised Him for His growing popularity with the people built a case against Him. They used their sway with the Romans, who were the governing principal in Jerusalem, calling for Jesus' execution. This was a practice the Roman hierarchy frequently used in their thrust for political order.

He knew it was coming! He told his disciples what would happen. He told them that He would be killed and buried, yes, but rise again in the resurrection–and that He would come again to receive us to himself for eternity. Let's be clear as to who gets this great gift.

In only a couple of sentences, John answers that question: "He was in the world, and the world was made through Him, and the world did not know Him. He came to His own and His own did not receive Him. But as many as received Him, to them He gave the right to become children of God . . ."

Jesus knew what His work would be. And, He knew He would die for what He came to the earth to accomplish. He knew that the purpose would be to shed His blood to provide a covering for the sins we commit. He taught us how to live in a kingdom that is different from the kingdom of the world. His kingdom is one of "righteousness, peace, and joy in the

Holy Spirit," (Romans 14:17). Here, we are children of God. "And, because you are sons, God has sent forth the Spirit of His Son into your hearts, crying out, "Abba, Father!" Therefore you are no longer a slave but a son, and if a son, then an heir of God through Christ," (Galatians 4:6-7).

We gradually learn how to live into the freedom this spiritual kingdom provides. No longer slaves to our sins, we move forward into our potential of becoming more fully human, fully alive.

The purpose of Jesus's sacrificial death is clear. It was a rescue mission! Open to all who want the light of Christ, which leads us to the Father, Creator God.

Good Friday's impact on life

With Easter on my mind I reminisce of a Good Friday of yesteryears, while Gary and I were raising three children on a tight budget. "Gary the Great" as I sometimes call him is speaking to our household of five.

"We need to tighten the belt, here." Belt? His words bring to mind the fact I have gained a few pounds—and I need to buy a new pair of jeans.

Always a writer, the following thoughts, recorded back then, were found today in my jammed-packed files:

"Making money stretch seems impossible. The car suddenly needs repairs, a wisdom tooth decides to raise its ugly head, and an insurance premium is due. It feels like the bills rule, here.

"I just yelled at my teenager for leaving the front door wide open, cooling the entire house. Dollar signs are seen in red. Then, when asked to drive nine miles out of my way to take a kid home who had stayed overnight, the needle on the gas gauge seems 10 foot tall.

"Good Friday finds me less than in a prayerful mood. Discouragement has come to spend the day. It's best I stop everything, read some Scriptures and pray. But now, to pick up the phone to stop the ringing.

"It's my friend, reminding me of this being Good Friday.

'Listen to this,' she says,' I found three Scripture for starting this amazing day.' (She sleeps late.)

"I didn't hear the second passage or the third, as the first verse struck a bullseye: "The wages of sin are death, but the free gift of God is eternal life." Yes, everything seems to cost. Expenses do win, sometimes, when push comes to shove. But here, in one short verse I see the Truth. The greatest of all gifts a believer ever receives is the gift of eternal life—and it's free! Given without a single fee—and tax free! There, simply to be cherished and received."

Yes. This day we call "Good Friday," allows us to once again rejoice in what Jesus, our Lord, has done for us. His destiny was known to Him. In a brutal process of being questioned and "tried," Jesus was given the opportunity to defend Himself before Herod Antipater, ruler of Galilee, and then by Pilate, procurator of Judea. With both, Jesus chose not to protect Himself. He knew by laying down His life for us He would become our Redeemer.

All who ask for forgiveness from sin receive His merciful touch on our lives. Restoration, lasting peace, joy and "right-doing" result.

Jesus said to look at the way the birds are cared for and to observe how beautifully the flowers are clothed. He promised to provide for us as we learn to trust. Sometimes, I think He looks at me and says, "Hey, you of little faith…." But, there is a smile on His face. Love is felt. When I truly seek to comprehend, I hears God's Holy Spirit speaking from within. Following His lead will see every genuine need is met.

It is easy to become so filled with the temporal—what's going on every day of our lives—that we cannot "see the Divine." Yes, there will always be bills, maybe more than can be paid. But fear, frustration and anxiety need not rob us of the peace intended, once we realize how loved we are.

Surely all the little creature comforts and all the things I think are needed will continue to take their hits, but God help me to remember all that is free: sunshine's warmth . . . a child's smile . . . a good night's sleep . . . the love of another . . . my very heartbeat. But the best is yet to come. Eternal life. All because one Good Friday, many lifetimes ago Jesus embraced the pain, the sorrow, the desolation and chose the cross. All because of us—and what we really need: peace and joy in the truth that the Lord Jesus has done so much for us. Undoubtedly, He is going to bring us through!

On counting our blessings . . .

Today, while on a walk with Gary, I recalled a spot where I fell some 20 years ago, having slipped on loose gravel at the corner of South Palo Verde and Fiesta Drive. Suddenly we hear the squeal of wheels—then the driver jumps out to help. He quickly tells us he is an ER doctor, here, visiting friends.

"I saw you fall!" After seeing where I was hurting, he said, "You may have a fractured rib; which can hurt a lot. You could go to the ER, yet this kind of fracture can heal by itself. It takes waiting it out."

Fortunately, we are close to home so it is not far to walk. Still, I can barely move for the pain. This is when Dr. "Good Heart" pulls a bottle of pills from his pocket, places a round, white pill in my hand and says, "This will help you until you can see your doctor." What he gave me was Tylenol #3-Codeine.

Even today, it is still hard to believe what happened. Not only the fact I stumbled over my own feet—but an emergency doctor stopped his car—"Johnny on the Spot"—to assess my status and provide a pain pill! Wow! Here is a good place to use of the word "awesome!" He was right, I only had a broken rib, but I think the experience of such amazing, sudden help was as good for me as the pill! This is an example of the kinds of things that don't reach the news.

Rarely do I have a low moment, but today I met with a wish for the world to stop so I could catch up. Gary said, "How about taking a nap. I think that will help." All I needed was that nudge. Upon awakening he suggested we take a walk and that is when he reminded me at the corner of "walk and don't walk" of what happened "way back when." I hope through the years this Good Samaritan has been blessed. Certainly, that is my prayer as for sure his name is still sacrosanct at our house!

Ours is a helping community and there seems to be good reason for that. I have heard stories of people who settled here at the community's earliest beginnings. Before there was a Kmart, or even a full-scale grocery store, people had to drive to Kingman for diapers and baby food. Those trips were shared as this made for less time and gas spent on the road for the many shopping events.

Imagine those early days when there was no hospital. So those early people, the true pioneers, were linked in spirit and cared very much about one another's needs. They put their "shoulder to the wheel" for the sake of others in ways that we can only imagine at this time. Love and gratitude surely flowed from house to house in many instances. This is a heritage, passed on to us.

Thanksgiving will soon be here. Many of us will be sitting at the table with loved ones, most likely thinking about that for which we are thankful. This is healthy—and it enriches our spirits. Those of us who read Scripture regularly know there are benefits in positive thinking, having a thankful heart—and looking for the good in all situations.

This wisdom is verified within many Scripture passages. For instance, Proverb 17:22, indicates gratitude even benefits our physical health: "A merry heart does good, *like* medicine, but a broken spirit dries the bones."

And, Proverbs 23:7, say, "For as he thinks in his heart, so is he . . ." Amazing as it may sound, our thoughts make us who we are.

Although sorrows do occur in life, we can alleviate the pain by choosing to perpetually revisit what is positive, and with faith perceive the good that lies ahead.

Remember the song . . . "Counting your many blessings, name them one by one . . . count your many blessings, see what God has done."

Parents say the darndest things!

My father-in-law, Harvey Smith, retired a few years ago. He finally has Sundays off and is free to go to church with his wife Helen. One Saturday night he telephoned. “Do you know that it’s hard work working for the Lord?” he said.

“What do you mean?” I asked.

“Well, I went to “Work Day’ at the church yesterday. I came home all sore and with aching muscles! Helen told me, “Don’t complain, you were working for the Lord.”

“I told her that it sure felt like I was working for Hap Whipple! That little man is so skinny he looks like the handle on the lawn mower I was pushing.” (Unlike us in Arizona, people in the Northwest have lawns.)

It didn’t quite ring true to Dad that Whipple, the straw boss of the day, could send several men twice his size home with aching muscles.

“I found out you get just as tired working for the Lord as you do working for yourself,” Dad said.

I laughed. But isn’t it true with all of us? We become enthused about doing something for God. We roll up our sleeves, plunge in, only to find it is hard work. Worse yet, sometimes there is opposition. The doors of success and progress still seem to move on creaking hinges—if they open at all. The romance of the thing goes out the window when the project does not roll out easily, the way “we” planned.

Meeting with rejection or criticism, we often respond with rebellion. “O.K., God, if that’s how they’re going to treat me, forget it! You can get someone else to do it.”

We want to be holy; we long to do what God asks of us. But we also want things to go our way. We want some appreciation and maybe a little recognition, right?

Jesus said, "Take my yoke upon your shoulders . . . my yoke is easy and my burden light." He also said to count the cost before starting to build. There seems to be a dichotomy here. Perhaps this can only be resolved by putting the whole picture together.

The Bible teaches us to link our lives with Christ through reading God's Word (the Bible). Doing so brings contentment, joy, great love and peace! Plus, assurance of eternal life! Jesus left what must have held "glorious splendors" in heaven to come to earth and become our Savior. He counted the cost and said "Yes."

At the beginning of Jesus' ministry there was a period of popularity. People flocked to see His miracles. But in comparison to the multitudes who came, only a handful were touched permanently by His love. Shortly, opposition set in. You know the story. Jesus followed the destiny laid out for Him to the grave. That is what He has called us to do.

Perhaps you or I will not be asked to die a martyr's death, but we have been commissioned to lay down our lives daily in the making of frequent choices—choices which embrace His will rather than our own. We are called to die to our preconceived ideas, to the desire to be appreciated and recognized, and to serve out of love alone.

When we have done our best to follow what we believe He has asked of us, then we meet with opposition. Solace comes in knowing that He, too, was criticized and misunderstood. Even the greatest gift mankind could ever receive—redemption through Christ's death on the cross—was not understood and appreciated by most. Jesus warned His followers not to expect better treatment.

So, how is it that His burden is light? It is light only when we embrace the truth of His having gone before us. He suffered in all ways that we do, even more! Yet, He conquered all!

As the apostle Paul wrote, "Yet, in all these things we are more than conquerors through Him who loved us," (Romans 8:37).

Conquerors are a particular brand of people, known for their ability to successfully overcome problems or weakness—even the most difficult of that which confronts us humans.

We know that within our life spans we will meet up with some times of frustration, disappointment, failures and physical difficulties. There are times of grief, even periods of sensing spiritual depletion, if only momentarily. What gives hope while we are feeling unsure, questioning or perplexed are passages like Romans 8:18-19, "For I consider that the sufferings of this present time are not worthy to be compared with the glory which shall be revealed in us. For the earnest expectation of the creation eagerly waits for the revealing of the sons of God."

There! We see what it means to be "more than conquerors," And—this is our quest!

About the Author

Joy Le Page Smith is a columnist with articles published in the US, England and Germany. This book carries the best of her newspaper columns published over the years. She has authored four books. Each will be described on the next two pages.

As a Board certified chaplain, she serves voluntarily at Havasu Regional Medical Center in Lake Havasu City and formerly in Phoenix, at Good Samaritan Regional Medical Center. For the past 25 years, Joy has served as a mental health provider and certified spiritual director in private practice. Her degrees are in psychology and theology.

Jail ministry and hospice chaplaincy "set her heart on fire" for doing what she could to bring the hope and comfort Jesus Christ offers within the Good News we find in the Scriptures. Jesus called it "the way" and said of Himself, "I am the way, the truth, and the life. No one comes to the Father except through Me," (John 14:6).

Joy's weekly column in Today's Herald-News, titled "By the Book" is based on life happenings that prove the worth of "the way." Her writings can create a desire for knowing more about the Scriptures.

The mission Joy embraces is that of being a loving, listening presence as she takes her faith to places of pain where individuals need hope, care and compassion.

As you read, feel free to write comments on Joy's interactive website. Comments can be placed at the bottom of any of her blogs at:

www.healinglifespain.com

Each of the chapters above, plus other books and articles can be found on the above site. Feel free to share these writings, while crediting the author's website.

Chaplain Joy Le Page Smith, M.A.

Mental Health Counselor – Author - Spiritual Mentor

Joy's books

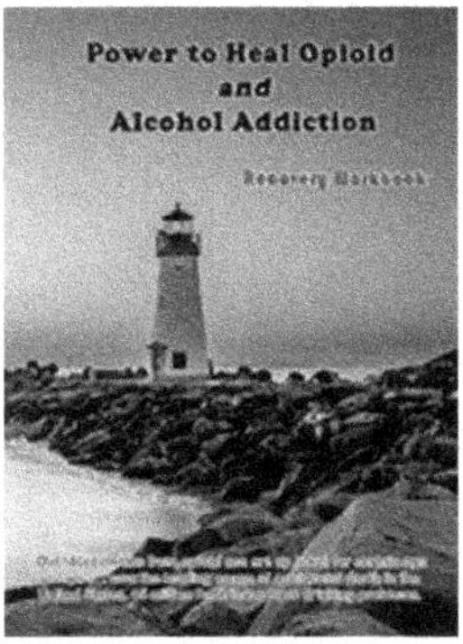

Power to Heal Opioid and Alcohol Addiction Recovery Workbook

Why Not Make the Trip Worthwhile?

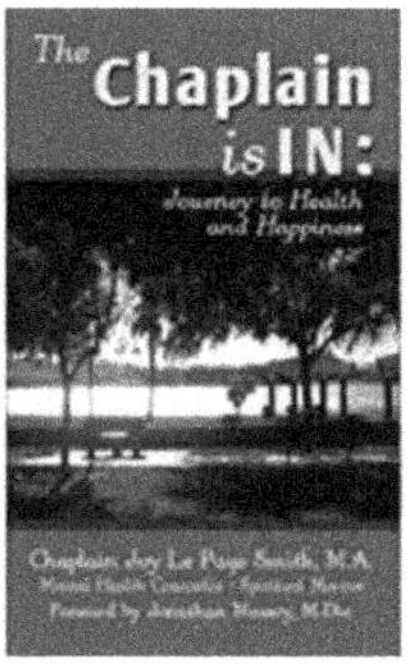

The Chaplain is In: Journey to Health and Happiness

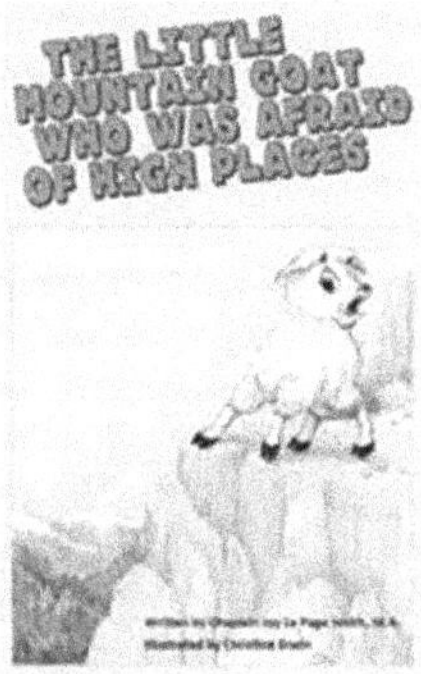

The Little Mountain Goat Who Was Afraid of High Places

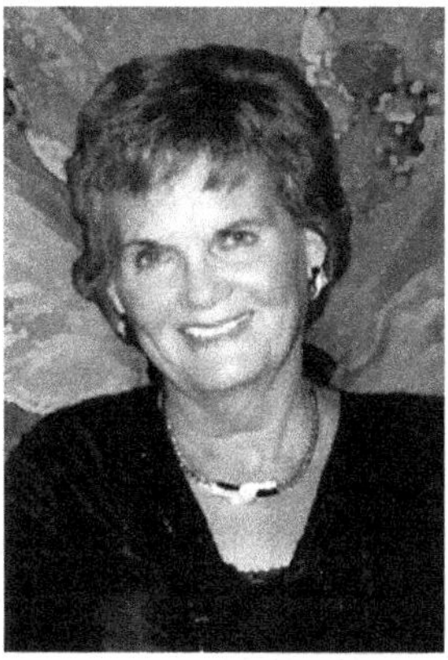

Taking care of oneself,

Body, mind and spirit,

Is one's best of all

Chance for health

And happiness, assuring

Furtherance of natural

Growth, exuberance,

Cheerfulness, brightness,

Hopefulness, and positive

Expectations for—

Good self-esteem and

Blessed accomplishments.

Books

By Joy Le Page Smith, MA, BCC

Available at:

www.healing-with-Joy.com

or

www.Healinglifespain.com

and

Amazon.com

Blogs and articles are available **free** at

www.healing-with-Joy.com

The "Quick Aids" button on website's homepage opens up numerous offerings and can be shared with others.

The sharing of Joy's website with others, is appreciated. Please *reference her website* in that event.

Listed, below are articles, prayers and other helps:

Help with Granting Forgiveness

Scriptures for When We are Afraid

Benefits for Those Who Have a Reverent Awe of God

Scriptures on Suffering

Scriptures for Times of Crisis

Dealing with Difficult Emotions - Finding Emotional Freedom

Tips for Teaching Children How to Identify What They Are Feeling

www.ingramcontent.com/pod-product-compliance
Lightning Source LLC
Chambersburg PA
CBHW060620070426
42446CB00052B/2791
9780692441244